GIFTS FROM
YOUR KITCHEN

GIFTS FROM YOUR KITCHEN

Georgia Chan Downard

Line Drawings by Mona Mark

NELSON DOUBLEDAY, INC.
Garden City, New York

TABLE OF CONTENTS
....

INTRODUCTION

Several years ago my husband and I decided to give a rather sumptuous Christmas party for a large group of friends. All being of a rather generous nature, next morning we found an array of surprises arranged beneath our tree. There were bottles of champagne and wine, an assortment of liqueurs and cordials, and some lovely Christmas ornaments. There was one gift, however, which invariably comes foremost to mind.

Nestled among the bottles and colorful Christmas wrappings was a small wooden mushroom basket. Lined with a red gingham napkin and cushioned with bright green tissue paper, it revealed a sparkling jar of apple butter tucked beside a loaf of fragrant oatmeal bread. These were accompanied by an antique cream bottle filled with homemade plum wine. Each was individually wrapped and lovingly prepared—the butter and wine months before, during the lazy days of summer, and the bread freshly baked on the morning of the party. I can still visualize that little basket with its treasure trove of goodies as if it were yesterday. It remains and forever shall be one of my most cherished gift memories.

I have always thought of the preparation of food for family and friends a natural extension of my love and affection for them. To my mind there is very little more special than receiving or being given a gift of food—a tailor-made surprise for a friend by one who cared enough to give generously in time and effort.

The words "homemade" and "homegrown" have taken on a very special meaning in today's world where most foods can be purchased in supermarkets or found in the myriad of specialty food shops which abound. No matter how well prepared and beautiful these mass-produced items may be, they will never take the place of something thoughtfully prepared at home with the particular preferences of a special someone in mind. Imagine the pure delight reflected in the eyes of a friend when presented with a miniature sack of chocolate bourbon balls. Months before he had intimated their place of importance in his reminiscences of childhood Christmases. His obvious pleasure in your thoughtfulness dispels any fears you may have had that the bourbon balls were not of uniform size and shape and that the wrapping paper wrinkled more than anticipated when being tied.

The many advantages in giving food gifts are numerous. The finest and freshest ingredients can be used and, most importantly, seasonal produce can be prepared at its peak and saved for those months when the scents and smells of a fragrant summer herb have faded into a pleasant memory. What could be more welcome to a holiday buffet than a pasta salad tossed with pesto sauce or a savory veal ragout flavored with the addition of a summer sorrel puree? Let the seasons help plan your holiday gift giving. Jams, marmalades, and pickles only improve with age as do fruitcakes and many confections. All can be prepared well in advance. It is even possible to have your Christmas gifts in order by the end of September. But please don't limit your gift giving to the holiday season. Birthdays, bridal showers, anniversaries, and picnics are just a few occasions when a gift of food might be welcome. There are many more.

The contribution of a sage-flavored pork tourtière to a hostess's weekend menu will not only ease her work load but will give her the opportunity to share, along with her guests, in all of the weekend's festivities. Simply check with her beforehand so that a complementary menu can result. If the menu plans are complete, select a gift which might be savored at a more private moment in days to come. A lovely crock filled with marinating goat cheese and sun-dried tomatoes can transform a simple afternoon repast into a culinary delight, especially when accompanied by a tin of sesame crackers. And what lovelier way to introduce yourself to new neighbors than with a pretty planter filled to overflowing with assorted homemade cookies? An overladen basket of scones might help ease the return home from a hospital stay for a friend who adores them, particularly if they are flavored with Cheddar cheese and accompanied by a jar of fig jam. Once you are in the habit of giving gifts of food it will become second nature.

The recipes following have been chosen with a number of considerations in mind. All are relatively easy to execute. Some may take a bit longer to prepare than others, but this is due to the addition of a few extra steps and not to the use of a particularly complicated technique. One need not hold a degree in advanced culinary arts to succeed and succeed quite well. All of the finished gifts can be transported with relative ease. In those cases where particular care is necessary, explicit instructions are given. The recipes are a mixture of time-honored classics and some comparatively new ideas—a combination which should appeal to everyone. And although they have not been divided into seasonal availability, the recipes should be viewed with an eye to taking advantage of each season's particular bounty—the time when certain foods can be purchased at their best and least expensive.

The most important consideration, however, is to enjoy yourself. My goal in presenting this book is to give you the opportunity to have fun in one of the most pleasurable ways possible. Motives need not be purely altruistic for, as trite as it sounds, it is truly in giving that we receive. If you derive just a small amount of the pleasure I have received in developing these recipes, then not only will you be happy but so will your friends, and in turn perhaps they will prepare and share similar gifts with others.

GEORGIA CHAN DOWNARD

GIFT WRAPS

....

The presentation of a gift of food should require no less thought and effort than that which went into its preparation. Of primary importance is that the gift wrap suit the article enclosed. Acting as an enhancement, it should never camouflage or overpower but simply adorn.

Fortunately there is almost a limitless supply of resources at hand for creating personalized gift wraps. Here are just a few you might consider:

Satin ribbons, colored yarns, and gold and silver flexible bands

Brightly patterned fabric samples, small swatches of lace, scraps of wallpaper, self-adhesive contact paper and sheets of colored tissue

Cut-out stencils of flowers, birds, hearts or whatever tickles your fancy—such is the stuff of which personalized gift wrapping is made

Cellophane is in and of itself an ideal wrap for baked goods and candies. Since it can be purchased in an assortment of colors, the food not only remains fresh but looks as festive as it is delicious to eat, especially when garnished with ribbon. In wrapping a loaf of bread be sure the cellophane is large enough to extend 4 to 5 inches at either end. Gently twist the ends and tie them closed with ribbon or yarn. Or form the cellophane into miniature sacks. Place a mound of candies or cookies in the center of a large sheet, gather the paper up over the candies and twist it to form a small bundle. Tie the bundle closed with a narrow ribbon or piece of yarn.

Containers

Empty tins with plastic tops, such as those containing coffee, shortening, and appetizers, can be stored away and used for these special gifts. They make ideal containers for a cluster of miniature macaroons, cookies, nuts, and snacks. Simply measure a piece of fabric or paper to fit the height and circumference of the tin, attach it with glue where necessary, and garnish the lid with a ribbon bow.

Preserving glasses and leftover jars with tight-fitting lids can be made to look special by topping with a piece of fabric or lace, trimmed with pinking shears 2 to 3 inches larger in diameter than the top of the jar. The fabric can be arranged over the lid and secured in place with a flexible band or ribbon.

Save mushroom baskets and small pint and quart fruit baskets, even the plastic ones. Painted, lined with a swatch of material or crisply starched napkin or tea towel, they become ideal receptacles for cookies, candies, and small cakes. What could be lovelier than a pint berry basket stuffed to capacity with individually wrapped toffees and benne brittle —all nestled on brightly colored tissue paper.

All cardboard boxes should be eyed with the possibility of housing a Bûche de Noël, a hazelnut

mocha cake or, better still, several dozen meringue kisses. Ideal for transporting cakes and pies, they are also very useful for fragile cookies and small cakes. The boxes can be lined with paper doilies. In the case of cookies or small cakes, additional doilies may act as cushioning between the layers. If the boxes are unmarked and a solid color, they need only the addition of one large or several small stenciled designs artfully arranged on the surface of the box. All other boxes can be wrapped in decorative paper and finished with ribbon bows, dried flowers, or yarn. When the lid entirely covers the top and sides of the box, only it need be wrapped. The box may then be saved and perhaps used again.

Good Sources

Flea markets, antique shops, and garage and tag sales are wonderful sources for unusual gift containers. These might include an English marmalade pot, an interestingly shaped antique bottle perfect for an herb vinegar or fruit syrup, a clear glass ginger jar or a large brandy snifter—both the ideal size for displaying an arrangement of layered candies and cookies. There are crocks, assorted china, tin and brass boxes, and serving bowls and dishes of all sizes and shapes to be found. Once unearthed, many can be bought for a song.

For That Special Gift

There may arise that very special occasion when the gift wrap itself forms a major part of the gift. A floral-design oven-to-table casserole containing a Greek pastitsio or a pretty pie plate filled with a pumpkin pecan chiffon pie would not only make lovely additions to a buffet table but be ideal gifts for a surprise birthday celebration.

A set of copper measuring cups containing a selection of compound butters, or a small silver bowl or candy dish filled to overflowing with champagne truffles—both are lovely ways of presenting very special gifts.

Porcelain and china ramekins, miniature soufflé dishes, dainty teacups and saucers, as well as more substantial earthenware mugs—all can be used inventively and will be a reminder of your thoughtfulness long after the food itself has disappeared.

These are only a few suggestions for the countless ways one can wrap a gift of food. Never again will you toss an empty shortening or coffee can into the trash bin before first checking your list of gift items. And don't be surprised if one evening you find yourself rummaging through the neighbor's pile of discarded cardboard boxes. There is no need for embarrassment—that little box may one day find itself under her Christmas tree, beautifully transformed into an imaginative gift wrap enveloping a gift from your kitchen.

And one more note—all gifts of food should be labeled and dated. Give instructions if the dish is to be defrosted or just reheated, served warm or cold. And when appropriate, list a few suggestions for serving, along with mention of complementary accompaniments.

GIFTS FROM
YOUR KITCHEN

APETIZERS AND
HORS D'OEUVRES

All of the recipes included here can be prepared several days
in advance and in most cases improve with age. Choosing the
appropriate wrap for each gift, however, is of particular importance not only for the sake of making it attractive but also for
preservation.

The spreads, dips, and pâtés will maintain their full fresh-
ness if stored in airtight containers and chilled well. Lovely
glass preserving jars, jelly glasses, and crocks are ideal containers not only for the items listed above but also for the mari-
nated goat cheese and egg plant caviar. Clear glass seems to
add to the appeal of the food. Garnish each container with a
swatch of fabric and attach it to the lid with a narrow ribbon
or plastic band.

The cayenne cheese straws are most successfully stored in
airtight tins. Used coffee or shortening tins with tight-fitting

1

lids are ideal. Simply cover with pretty wrapping paper or contact paper, or glue a piece of fabric onto the outside of the tin and top the lid with a bow.

As for the Gorgonzola and Mascarpone walnut roll, enclose it first in plastic wrap and then in colored cellophane, being sure the cellophane extends at either end by several inches, and tie the ends closed with ribbon or string.

Gorgonzola and Mascarpone Walnut Roll

1/4 pound Gorgonzola cheese	1/2 pound Mascarpone cheese
1/2 cup (1 stick) unsalted butter, softened	1/2 cup chopped walnuts

Combine Gorgonzola and butter in processor and process until smooth. Spread the mixture into a 7-inch square on a piece of wax paper and cover the Gorgonzola with the Mascarpone, smoothing it into an even layer. Chill the cheese, covered, for 10 minutes or until the cheese is firm but still pliable. Roll up the cheese, jelly-roll fashion, to form a log, and sprinkle it with the walnuts, pressing them into the surface of the cheese. Chill the log, covered, for at least 2 hours or overnight. Serve the cheese slightly chilled, accompanied by crackers. Makes a 1-pound log.

Sesame Chick-Pea Dip
(Hummus bi Tahini)

2 cups cooked or canned
  chick-peas, reserving 2
  tablespoons of the
  liquid
2 cloves garlic
1/3 cup lemon juice

1/3 cup sesame seed
  paste
1/3 cup olive oil
1/2 teaspoon salt
Freshly ground pepper

Combine all the ingredients in a food processor or blender and puree until smooth. Turn into a serving dish or container and chill, covered, for at least 2 hours or overnight. Serve at room temperature, garnished with black olives, minced parsley, and a sprinkling of olive oil. Accompany with pita triangles. Makes about 2 1/2 cups.

The dip will keep, covered and chilled, for up to 1 week.

Herbed Tomato and Olive Loaf
(Pan Bagnat)

1 loaf Italian whole wheat or French bread, 16 inches long

3 large tomatoes, peeled, seeded, and chopped

1/4 cup minced scallions, including green tops

1/4 cup minced green pepper

10 pimiento-stuffed olives, chopped

10 Kalamata or similar black olives, pitted and chopped

1/4 cup minced parsley

3 tablespoons grated Parmesan cheese

1 tablespoon drained capers

2 tablespoons minced fresh basil or 1/2 teaspoon dried

1 teaspoon salt

1/4 teaspoon dried thyme

Lemon juice to taste

3 to 4 tablespoons olive oil

Cut off the ends of the bread, slice open lengthwise leaving top and bottom attached, and hollow out center, reserving the crumbs, and forming a 1/4-inch-thick shell. Chop the crumbs (there should be 2 cups) and combine with the remaining ingredients, adding enough oil to hold the mixture together. The filling should be highly seasoned. Spoon into bottom of shell, spread into even layer, reform into loaf, and wrap tightly in plastic wrap and foil. Chill overnight. Serve cut into slices. Serves 6 to 8.

This is jocularly known as Poor Man's Caviar.

Eggplant Caviar Dip

1 medium eggplant
  (about 1 pound)
2 scallions, minced
1 medium clove garlic,
  minced
2 tablespoons lemon
  juice

2 tablespoons imported
  sesame oil
2 tablespoons olive oil
1/2 teaspoon salt
Freshly ground pepper
3 tablespoons minced
  parsley

Pierce the eggplant with a knife and bake at 350° F. for 1 hour or until tender. Let cool. Combine eggplant pulp, chopped fine, with remaining ingredients and spoon into a glass jar or container. Chill the dip for 2 hours or overnight. Serve at room temperature, garnished with sliced tomatoes and black olives. Accompany with pita triangles. Makes 1 cup.

Marinated Goat Cheese
with Sun-Dried Tomatoes

1 1/2 cups olive oil
1/2 cup dry white wine
2 cloves garlic, sliced
1 teaspoon black
    peppercorns
1 teaspoon dried basil
1/2 teaspoon dried thyme
1/2 teaspoon dried
    oregano
1 bay leaf
1 strip lemon peel

1 teaspoon salt
1/4 pound sun-dried
    tomatoes
1/2 pound goat cheese in
    1 piece, or 3 small
    rounds such as Crottin
    de Chavignol
3 tablespoons minced
    parsley
3 tablespoons snipped
    chives

Put the oil, wine, garlic, peppercorns, basil, thyme, oregano, bay leaf, lemon peel, and salt into a saucepan, bring to a boil and add tomatoes. Simmer for 10 minutes or until tomatoes are tender and cool. Arrange tomatoes and cheese in a crock or jar. Sprinkle with the fresh herbs and cover with oil, adding more oil, if necessary, to completely cover the ingredients. Store in the refrigerator, covered, for at least 1 week before serving. Serve at room temperature. Reserve the marinade for use in salad dressings.

YOU CAN MAKE THIS AHEAD. THE CHEESE WILL KEEP, COVERED AND CHILLED, UP TO 6 WEEKS.

Apple and Chicken Liver Pâté
with Hazelnuts

10 tablespoons (1¼ sticks) unsalted butter, softened

2 medium Granny Smith apples, peeled, cored, and chopped

1 large onion, chopped

6 juniper berries, crushed

¼ teaspoon dried thyme

¼ teaspoon dried sage

1 large clove garlic, minced

1 pound chicken livers, rinsed and patted dry

¼ cup Sercial Madeira or dry sherry

4 tablespoons heavy cream

Freshly grated nutmeg to taste

Salt and pepper to taste

½ cup chopped toasted hazelnuts

In a large saucepan melt 4 tablespoons of the butter and cook the apples and onions seasoned with juniper, thyme, and sage over moderate heat, covered, stirring occasionally, for 8 to 10 minutes or until the vegetables are soft. Add the garlic and cook over moderate heat, stirring, for 1 minute. Transfer to a processor or blender and puree until smooth. Add 2 tablespoons of butter to pan and sauté the livers until they are browned on the outside but still pink within; transfer to processor. Deglaze the pan with the Madeira and reduce it to 2 tablespoons. Add Madeira to processor, puree until mixture is smooth and let cool for 10 minutes. With the motor running add the remaining 4 tablespoons butter, 1 tablespoon at a time, the heavy cream, nutmeg, and salt and pepper to taste. Fold in the hazelnuts, spoon the pâté into a crock or serving dish, and chill overnight. Serve at room temperature garnished with a preserved crab apple and hazelnuts. Makes about 3 cups. The pâté will keep, covered and chilled, for 1 week.

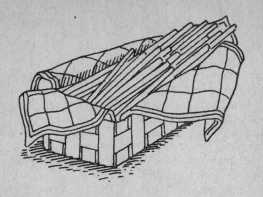

Perfect as an accompaniment to cocktails before dinner —enough to tease the palate without overshadowing the main event.

Cayenne Cheese Straws

1½ cups flour
1⅛ teaspoons salt
½ teaspoon cayenne pepper
½ cup cold unsalted butter, cut into bits
¼ pound sharp Cheddar cheese, grated

1 egg, separated
3 to 4 tablespoons ice water
Worcestershire sauce to taste
Poppy seeds to taste

Sift the flour, 1 teaspoon of the salt, and cayenne. Add butter and cut in until the mixture resembles coarse meal. Add the cheese. Beat egg yolk with ice water and Worcestershire sauce, toss with the flour mixture and form into a ball. (The dough may sit covered and chilled overnight.) Knead lightly with the heel of a hand to distribute butter, reform into a ball and chill, covered,

8

for 1 hour. Beat egg white with 2 teaspoons water and remaining salt. Roll dough between sheets of wax paper into a 1/4-inch-thick rectangle, brush with the glaze and sprinkle with poppy seeds. Cut dough into strips about 5 × 1/4 × 1/4 inches. Arrange on buttered baking sheets and bake in a preheated 400° F. oven for 12 to 15 minutes or until golden. Let cool on racks. Stored in airtight containers, the straws will keep for 2 weeks. Makes about 60.

A lovely, somewhat extravagant gift, the salmon should be presented in fittingly appropriate wrappings. A china or pretty earthenware crock would do beautifully—simply garnish with a satin ribbon bow tied under the rim of the crock.

Potted Smoked Salmon

1 1/2 pounds fresh salmon
2 tablespoons dry white wine
2 tablespoons minced shallots
1 bay leaf
1 teaspoon salt
White pepper to taste
1/8 teaspoon ground cloves
1/8 teaspoon mace
3/4 cup unsalted butter, softened

1/2 pound smoked salmon, cut into 1-inch pieces
Salt and white pepper to taste
1/3 cup clarified butter made by melting 1/2 cup, skimming off the top, and straining through a double thickness of cheesecloth

Arrange the salmon in a buttered baking pan just large enough to hold it, sprinkle with wine and shallots and

9

season with bay leaf, salt, pepper, cloves, and mace. Cut 1/4 cup of the butter into pats and arrange over salmon.

Bake, covered, in a 350° F. oven for 45 to 50 minutes, or until the fish flakes easily. Let cool to room temperature. Skin, bone, and flake the salmon, and strain the cooking liquid into a blender or food processor. Add the salmon, blend until smooth, and with the motor running add the remaining butter, 1 tablespoon at a time, until the mixture is smooth. Transfer to a bowl. Add the smoked salmon to blender and puree. Beat the smoked salmon into the fresh salmon mixture, season with salt and white pepper to taste, and transfer to a terrine or crock.

Cover with clarified butter and plastic wrap and chill overnight. The salmon will keep, covered and chilled with the seal unbroken, for up to one week. Suggest serving the salmon at room temperature with whole wheat crackers or thin dark bread. Makes 3 1/2 cups.

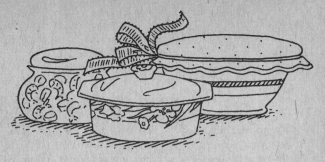

ENTREES

· ·

Included in this section are a number of casseroles and salads
which can be prepared in advance, are easy to transport, and
can be attractively presented. In many instances, it may be
more advantageous to present the casseroles unbaked, with
instructions attached for baking (include oven temperatures
and cooking times).

Ideal gifts for a weekend host or hostess and festive additions to a buffet table, the casseroles may be presented in
attractive oven-to-table baking dishes or simple heatproof glass
dishes. In the case of an outdoor bazaar or church supper
when informality reigns, one of the many aluminum foil baking dishes available at supermarkets and grocery stores would
be quite acceptable. Let the particular occasion dictate the
elaborateness of the gift wrap.

The salads are best presented in clear glass bowls or platters.
That is not to say, however, that they wouldn't look just as
lovely on china or silver. Again it depends upon the occasion
and your generosity.

Be sure all are covered with plastic or foil and kept chilled
until transported and served.

11

Topped with mashed potatoes, this is a complete meal in and of itself. Consider it when introducing yourself to new neighbors or when welcoming home a friend from a hospital stay. In my opinion, it is true comfort food.

English Seafood Pie

9 tablespoons unsalted butter
1 cup minced onions
1/2 cup sliced celery
1/3 cup minced carrots
1/4 pound mushrooms, sliced
1 cup bottled clam juice
1/2 cup dry white wine or dry vermouth
Bouquet garni (cheesecloth bag containing 12 parsley stems, 1 teaspoon dried thyme, 6 peppercorns, and 1 bay leaf)
1 pound large shrimp, shelled, deveined, and halved lengthwise
1/2 pound sea scallops, halved if large
3/4 pound cod
1 1/2 cups milk
4 tablespoons flour
1/4 cup heavy cream
1/4 cup freshly grated Parmesan cheese
1/4 cup minced fresh parsley
2 teaspoons Dijon-style mustard
freshly grated nutmeg to taste
lemon juice to taste
Salt and pepper to taste

For the topping:
2 1/2 pounds baking potatoes
3/4 cup cream or milk
4 tablespoons unsalted butter
Salt and pepper to taste
1 tablespoon bread crumbs
1 tablespoon Parmesan cheese
Paprika to taste
3 tablespoons melted unsalted butter

Melt 3 tablespoons of the butter over moderately low heat and cook the onions, celery, carrots, and mushrooms, covered, for 8 to 10 minutes or until the onion is soft. Add the clam juice, the wine, and the bouquet garni. Bring to a simmer and stir in the shellfish. Bring back to a simmer, stirring, and remove pan from heat.

In a shallow baking dish poach the cod in the milk seasoned with salt and pepper over low heat for 5 minutes, or just until it flakes when tested with a fork. With a slotted spoon transfer the cod to a dish, reserving the milk, and let cool. Skin, bone, and flake the cod and transfer to a bowl. Drain the shellfish and vegetables, reserving the liquid and cheesecloth bag, and add to the bowl containing the cod. Combine the poaching liquids and add enough water to measure 3 1/2 cups.

In a saucepan melt the remaining butter, add the flour and cook over moderately low heat, stirring, for 3 minutes. Add the reserved liquid and cheesecloth bag and simmer, stirring occasionally, for 20 minutes. Remove cheesecloth bag. Strain through a fine sieve into a bowl and add the heavy cream, cheese, parsley, mustard, nutmeg, lemon juice, and salt and pepper. Combine the shellfish and cod with the sauce and correct seasoning. Transfer to a buttered baking dish.

Make the topping: Bake the potatoes in a 400° F. oven for 1 hour or until tender. Remove from skins and whip with the cream or milk, butter, and salt and pepper. Transfer to a pastry bag fitted with a large decorative tip and pipe on top of seafood. Sprinkle with the bread crumbs, cheese, paprika, and melted butter. The pie may be assembled to this point and kept covered and chilled overnight. Bake the pie in a 400° F. oven for 30 to 35 minutes, or until it is golden brown on top. Serves 6 to 8.

THIS PIE MAY ALSO BE ASSEMBLED, KEPT COVERED AND CHILLED, AND GIVEN WITH COOKING INSTRUCTIONS.

Of French-Canadian origin, Tourtière is traditionally served after midnight Mass on Christmas Eve (Réveillon) or on Christmas day. My adaptation may be served either warm or at room temperature. With the simple addition of a crisp green salad, it makes a wonderful hearty luncheon entrée and is perfect for picnics and buffets.

French-Canadian Tourtière

For the pastry:

2 cups all-purpose flour
1/2 teaspoon salt
10 tablespoons cold unsalted butter, cut into pieces

3 tablespoons cold lard or vegetable shortening
4 to 5 tablespoons ice water

2 cups minced onions
2 tablespoons unsalted butter
1 tablespoon olive oil
2 pounds lean ground pork
3 to 4 garlic cloves, minced
1 teaspoon dried thyme
1/2 teaspoon dried sage
1/2 teaspoon ground allspice
1 bay leaf
1/2 cup dry white wine
1/2 cup beef broth

1 cup chopped tomatoes, well drained
2 tablespoons tomato paste
1/2 teaspoon salt
1/4 teaspoon pepper
3 tablespoons minced fresh parsley
1 egg beaten with 2 tablespoons heavy cream
An egg wash made by beating 1 egg with 2 teaspoons water and a pinch of salt

Make the pastry: Sift flour and salt, cut in butter and lard until mixture resembles coarse meal. Add ice water, tossing the mixture until the liquid is incorporated and

15

form it into a ball. Divide dough into two flattened balls, one slightly larger than the other, and chill, wrapped in wax paper, for 1 hour.

Cook the onions in the butter and oil, stirring, until softened. Add pork and cook until it is no longer pink. Stir in garlic and dried herbs, cook 1 minute, and add wine. Reduce until almost completely evaporated, add broth and reduce by half. Stir in tomatoes, tomato paste, and salt and pepper and simmer until thick. Let cool for 30 minutes and remove bay leaf.

Roll out smaller round of dough 1/8 inch thick and fit into a 9-inch piepan, trimming the edge to form a 1/2-inch overhang. Brush with egg wash, prick bottom and spread pork mixture in shell, mounding it slightly. Roll out remaining dough 1/8 inch thick and drape over filling. Trim top crust, leaving a 1-inch overhang; fold under bottom crust and crimp edge decoratively. Make slits in top crust for steam vents and brush dough with egg wash. Bake on a baking sheet in a 450° F. oven for 10 minutes, then reduce to 350° and bake 40 minutes longer or until crust is golden. Serves 4 to 6 as an entrée, 8 to 10 as an hors d'oeuvre.

Coming to us from Greece, this is a slightly different and perfect party dish. If kept covered and chilled, it easily can be assembled a day or even two ahead of time before baking.

Pastitsio

For the filling:

2 1/2 cups minced onions

2 tablespoons unsalted butter

2 1/2 pounds ground lean lamb

1/2 teaspoon salt

1/4 teaspoon pepper

3 garlic cloves, minced
1/2 cup dry white wine
1 can (1 pound, 12 ounces) tomatoes, pureed with the liquid
3 tablespoons tomato paste

1 1/2 teaspoons cinnamon
1 teaspoon dried basil
1 teaspoon dried thyme
1 teaspoon dried rosemary
1 bay leaf

For the white sauce:
4 tablespoons unsalted butter

4 tablespoons flour
3 cups milk, scalded

6 cups cooked macaroni (about 12 ounces uncooked)
6 tablespoons unsalted butter, softened
1 cup freshly grated Parmesan cheese

2 eggs, beaten lightly
Salt and pepper to taste
1/3 cup bread crumbs

Make the filling: In a large skillet or saucepan, cook the onions in the butter until softened. Add the lamb seasoned with the salt and pepper and cook until it is no longer pink. Add the garlic, cook 1 minute, and pour off fat from pan. Add the wine, reduce for 1 minute, and stir in remaining ingredients. Simmer covered, stirring occasionally, for 20 minutes or until thickened. Remove bay leaf and let cool.

Make the white sauce: In a saucepan melt the butter, add flour and cook, stirring, over low heat for 3 minutes. Add milk, bring to a boil, whisking, and simmer 15 minutes.

Combine the macaroni, 4 tablespoons of the butter, 1/2 cup of the cheese, the eggs, and salt and pepper to taste.

Spoon half the macaroni into a large shallow baking dish, add half the meat filling and cover with the remaining macaroni and meat. Spoon white sauce over the top, cover with the remaining Parmesan and the bread crumbs, and dot with the remaining butter. Bake in a preheated 400° F. oven for 40 to 50 minutes or until the top is golden and the filling is bubbling. Serves 6 to 8.

YOU CAN TAKE THIS TO YOUR HOSTESS, CHILLED AND WITH A NOTE FOR BAKING INSTRUCTIONS.

The popularity of Southwestern dishes has risen enormously over the past few years and continues on the rise —as well it should. This casserole combines some of the more distinctive elements of the cuisine, including chilies, cheese, and tortillas. All combine to make it a wonderfully flavorful dish.

Southwestern Chicken and Tortilla Casserole

For the sauce:

4 tablespoons unsalted butter
4 tablespoons flour
2 1/2 cups chicken broth
1 cup milk
1/4 teaspoon salt

1/8 teaspoon pepper
1/2 cup sour cream
1/4 teaspoon cayenne pepper
1/4 teaspoon chili powder (optional)

1 1/2 cups minced onions
1/2 pound mushrooms, sliced
1 red bell pepper, minced

3 tablespoons unsalted butter
1 cup chopped tomatoes, well drained
2 garlic cloves, minced

18

1 teaspoon ground
  cumin
1/4 teaspoon salt
1/8 teaspoon pepper
3 medium-hot canned or
  bottled chilies or
  jalapeño peppers, or to
  taste
3 tablespoons minced
  fresh coriander
  (optional)

12 corn tortillas,
  softened for 1 minute
  in hot vegetable oil
4 cups chopped cooked
  chicken
1 pound Monterey Jack
  cheese, grated

Make the sauce: In a saucepan melt the butter over low
heat, add the flour and cook the mixture, stirring, for 3
minutes. Add the chicken stock, milk, and salt and pepper to taste and simmer the sauce, stirring occasionally,
for 20 minutes. Let the sauce cool for 10 minutes, stir in
the sour cream, cayenne, and chili powder.

In a saucepan cook the onions, mushrooms, and red pepper in the butter, stirring, until the onions are softened.
Add the tomatoes, garlic, cumin, and salt and pepper
and cook the mixture over moderate heat, stirring, until
almost all the liquid has evaporated. Add the chilies or
jalapeño peppers, minced, and the coriander.

Line a well-buttered 3-quart baking dish with half the
tortillas so that they come halfway up the sides of
the pan, cover with half of the chicken, and spoon 1/3 of
the sauce over the chicken. Add half the cheese, half the
vegetables, and 1/3 more sauce. Repeat with the remaining tortillas, chicken, sauce, vegetables, and cheese. The
dish may be assembled ahead to this point and kept
covered and chilled overnight. Bake in a 350° F. oven for
45 to 55 minutes or until the top is lightly golden and
the filling bubbling. Serves 6.

THIS CASSEROLE MAY BE ASSEMBLED, COVERED AND CHILLED, AND GIVEN WITH COOKING INSTRUCTIONS, IF YOU WISH.

One of my very favorite seafood salads, this is light, refreshing, and can be prepared completely in advance. Served on soft-leaf lettuce and accompanied by crusty Italian bread, it can be the perfect repast for a summer's day or the night before Christmas, when some traditions dictate seafood as dinner fare. Think about it as a hostess gift for a tree-trimming party. It's very transportable and in another season would be great beach or picnic fare.

Insalata di Frutti di Mare
(Italian Seafood Salad)

For the dressing:

1/3 cup lemon juice

1 tablespoon Dijon-style mustard

2 garlic cloves, minced

1/2 teaspoon salt

1/4 teaspoon pepper

1 cup olive oil

1/4 cup minced fresh parsley

2 tablespoons snipped fresh dill

2 dozen mussels, cleaned

2/3 cup dry white wine

Bouquet garni (cheesecloth bag containing 12 parsley stems, 1 teaspoon dried thyme, 1 bay leaf and 6 peppercorns)

Salt and pepper to taste

1 pound bay scallops

1 pound squid (calamari), cleaned, the body sacs and flaps cut crosswise into 1/4-inch slices and the tentacles cut crosswise into 1-inch pieces

20

1 pound large shrimp,
  shelled and deveined
1 cup minced red pepper
1 cup sliced fennel
1 small red onion, sliced
  thin

8 to 12 oil-cured or
  kalamata olives, pitted
  and halved

Make the dressing: Combine the lemon juice, mustard, garlic, and salt and pepper in a blender and blend until smooth. With the motor running, add the oil and blend until combined well. Add the parsley and dill.

In a large kettle combine the mussels, wine, and bouquet garni. Bring to a boil and steam, covered, for 5 to 7 minutes or until the shells have opened. With a slotted spoon transfer to a large bowl, reserving cooking liquid; cool and shell. In a large ceramic or glass bowl toss the mussels with the dressing.

Remove and reserve the bouquet garni. Strain the cooking liquid through a fine sieve lined with a double thickness of rinsed and squeezed cheesecloth and add enough water to measure 2½ cups. Bring liquid to a simmer, add bouquet garni and salt and pepper and poach the scallops and squid for 1 to 2 minutes or until opaque. With a slotted spoon transfer the seafood to the bowl and toss. Bring cooking liquid to a simmer, add shrimp and poach 2 to 3 minutes or until firm. Transfer with a slotted spoon to the bowl, toss the mixture well and chill it, covered, for at least 2 hours or overnight. Add the remaining ingredients and toss the salad gently until it is combined well. Serve on soft-leaf lettuce garnished with arugula leaves, if desired, at room temperature. Serves 4 to 6.

Although at its best when prepared with fresh spring vegetables, this salad can be made year round simply by taking advantage of the seasonal produce available. Use your imagination and personal preferences in selecting the vegetables, with particular attention to colors. If tortellini is not available, any macaroni-type pasta will do. Another dish that is wonderfully transportable. Excellent for the beach or picnics.

Tortellini Salad Primavera

1 pound cheese or meat tortellini
1 cup cooked peas
1/4 pound cooked green beans or snow peas
1 summer squash, sliced and blanched

1/4 pound button mushrooms, sliced if large
1 red pepper, minced
1/2 teaspoon salt
1/4 teaspoon pepper
3 tablespoons olive oil

For the dressing:
1 egg
1 egg yolk
3 tablespoons lemon juice
2 tablespoons white wine vinegar
1 tablespoon Dijon-style mustard

1 large shallot, chopped
1 cup olive oil
3 tablespoons sour cream
1/3 cup chopped fresh basil or parsley
Salt and pepper to taste

Cook the tortellini in boiling salted water until tender; drain, and refresh under cold water. In a large bowl combine tortellini, peas, beans, squash, mushrooms, peppers, and salt and pepper. Add olive oil and toss to coat ingredients. Cover and chill if not serving immediately.

Make the dressing: Combine all ingredients except oil, sour cream, and basil in blender or food processor and blend. With the motor running add oil, sour cream, basil, and salt and pepper. Serve the salad at room temperature, tossed with the dressing. Serves 6 to 8.

A beautiful way to present this salad is with a garniture of fruit. Arrange the salad in the center of a large platter and surround it with clusters of grapes, apple slices, and orange segments. Not only lovely to behold but very refreshing and satisfying.

Curried Turkey Rice Salad

1 onion, quartered
1 small carrot, chopped
1/2 celery stalk, chopped
1 teaspoon dried thyme
6 peppercorns
3 whole cloves
1 small bay leaf
6 parsley sprigs
1 cup chicken broth
2 cups water or enough to cover turkey
1 (2-pound) turkey

breast with rib cage attached
4 cups cooked rice, cooled
1 cup raisins
1 cup coarsely chopped nuts such as walnuts, cashews, or almonds
1 red pepper, minced
4 tablespoons minced fresh coriander (optional)

For the dressing:
1 egg
1 egg yolk
2 tablespoons lemon juice
2 tablespoons white wine vinegar
1 tablespoon Dijon-style mustard
2 1/2 teaspoons curry powder, or to taste

1 small garlic clove, chopped (optional)
1 small onion, chopped
Salt and pepper to taste
3/4 cup olive oil
1/2 cup vegetable oil
1/2 cup plain yogurt
Fresh sprigs of coriander for garnish (optional)

In a saucepan combine onions, carrots, celery, herbs, chicken broth, and water; bring to a boil and add turkey. Simmer, partially covered, for 30 minutes or until tender. Uncover and let turkey cool in liquid. Remove meat from bones and cut into bite-size pieces. In a large bowl combine the turkey, rice, raisins, nuts, red pepper, and coriander.

Make the dressing: In a blender combine the egg, yolk, lemon juice, vinegar, mustard, curry powder, garlic, onions, and salt and pepper and blend until smooth. With the motor running add the oils in a stream, and then the yogurt. Blend the dressing until combined well. Toss the salad with the dressing and garnish with the coriander. Serves 6 to 8.

BREADS

•••

You will find an assortment of holiday breads in this section as well as a number of all-purpose and versatile favorites. The scones, muffins, and corn bread are best eaten when warm; there are specific instructions in each recipe for reheating. All of the breads included are delicious when toasted, and therefore can be enjoyed for several days if wrapped in plastic.

Cellophane is the most practical and colorful gift wrap. Center bread loaves on large pieces of cellophane, being sure the cellophane extends several inches at either end, and twist and tie the ends together with ribbon or string. Wooden boards are attractive foundations for baked goods, as are napkin-lined baskets of all shapes and sizes. In the case of the chili cheese corn bread, why even remove it from the old-fashioned black iron skillet in which it was baked—a charming, inexpensive, and totally practical gift wrap.

Greek Easter Bread

1 1/2 cups lukewarm milk
2 tablespoons active-dry yeast
1/4 cup plus 1 teaspoon sugar
2 eggs, beaten lightly
1 tablespoon grated orange peel
1 teaspoon grated lemon peel
1 teaspoon salt
1/2 cup softened unsalted butter

5 1/2 to 6 cups all-purpose flour
4 hard-boiled eggs, colored red
1 tablespoon sesame seeds
An egg wash made by beating 1 egg with 2 teaspoons water and a pinch of salt

Proof yeast with 1/2 cup of milk and 1 teaspoon sugar for 15 minutes or until foamy. In a bowl combine remaining milk, eggs, orange and lemon peels, salt, remaining sugar, and butter. Stir in 5 1/2 cups flour, or enough to form a soft but not sticky dough. Transfer to floured surface and knead, incorporating more flour if necessary, for 8 to 10 minutes or until smooth. Form into a ball, put in a buttered bowl and turn it to coat with butter. Let dough rise, covered with plastic wrap and a dish towel, for 1 1/2 hours or until double in bulk. Punch down, divide into three, and form each third into a rope about 18 inches long. Braid the ropes and form braid into a round, pinching the ends together. Transfer to a buttered baking sheet and arrange eggs in braids. Let the loaf rise, loosely covered, for 3/4 to 1 hour or until almost doubled in bulk. Brush loaf with the glaze and sprinkle with sesame seeds. Bake in a 375° F. oven for 45 minutes or until it sounds hollow when the bottom is tapped. Transfer to a rack and let cool.

Should you have access to walnut oil, an expensive and sometimes difficult to find item, try substituting the oil for all or half of the butter. The end result will be a very light whole wheat bread with the intense flavor of walnuts.

Whole Wheat Walnut Bread

2 tablespoons active-dry
  yeast
1¼ cups lukewarm
  water
1 teaspoon sugar
1 cup milk
4 tablespoons light
  molasses, unsulfured
6 tablespoons unsalted
  butter, softened

1 teaspoon salt
3 cups whole wheat flour
3½ to 4 cups all-purpose
  unbleached flour
1 cup chopped walnuts
An egg wash made by
  beating 1 egg with 2
  teaspoons water and a
  pinch of salt

In a large bowl proof the yeast in ½ cup of the water with the sugar for 15 minutes or until foamy. In a bowl combine the milk, molasses, butter, and salt and add to yeast mixture. Stir in the whole wheat flour and 3 cups of the unbleached flour. Transfer dough to a floured surface and knead it, incorporating more unbleached flour if the dough is too sticky, for 8 to 10 minutes or until smooth. Form the dough into a ball, put it into a buttered bowl and turn it to coat it with the butter. Cover the bowl with plastic wrap and a dish towel and let the dough rise for 1½ hours or until doubled in bulk. Punch down dough and knead in walnuts. Halve dough, form each half into a loaf, and put the loaves in two buttered loaf pans, 8½ × 4½ × 2⅝ inches. Let the loaves rise, covered loosely, for 45 minutes or until they have risen 1½ inches above the rims of the loaf pans. Brush with the glaze and bake in a 400° F. oven for 45 minutes, or until the loaves sound hollow when the bottoms are tapped. Transfer to racks to cool for 10 minutes, turn out onto racks and let cool completely. Makes 2 loaves.

This bread has a lovely texture—particularly suited to sandwiches and to toasting. It would be a dandy addition to any picnic hamper.

Caraway Rye Bread

2 tablespoons active-dry
  yeast
1½ cups lukewarm milk
1 teaspoon sugar
2 tablespoons light
  molasses, unsulfured
2 teaspoons salt

2 teaspoons caraway
  seeds
1½ cups whole wheat
  flour
1 cup rye flour
1½ to 2 cups all-purpose
  unbleached flour

In a large bowl proof the yeast in ½ cup of the milk with the sugar for 15 minutes or until foamy. In a small bowl combine the remaining milk, molasses, salt, and caraway, and add to the yeast mixture. Stir in the whole wheat flour, the rye flour, and 1½ cups of the unbleached flour. Transfer the dough to a floured surface and knead it, incorporating more unbleached flour if the dough is too sticky, for 8 to 10 minutes or until smooth. Form into a ball, put in a buttered bowl and turn it to coat with the butter. Cover the bowl with plastic wrap and a dish towel and let the dough rise for 1½ hours or until doubled in bulk. Punch down dough and knead lightly. Form the dough into a round and transfer to a buttered baking sheet. Let the loaf rise, covered loosely, for 30 minutes or until almost doubled. Brush the loaf with water and bake in a 400° F. oven for 15 minutes, or until it sounds hollow when the bottom is tapped. Transfer to a rack and let cool completely. Makes 1 loaf.

These are delicate sweet rolls similar to English tea cakes and, like them, perfect for tea or toasted for breakfast.

Butternut Squash Rolls

1 (1-pound) butternut squash
2 tablespoons active-dry yeast
1/4 cup warm orange juice
1 teaspoon sugar
1 cup milk
1 cup currants
5 tablespoons light brown sugar
5 tablespoons unsalted butter, melted and cooled

1 egg, beaten lightly
1 tablespoon grated orange peel
11/2 teaspoons salt
1/2 teaspoon cinnamon
1/4 teaspoon mace
1/4 teaspoon ginger
7 to 8 cups all-purpose unbleached flour
An egg wash made by beating 1 egg with 2 teaspoons water and a pinch of salt

Bake the squash on an oiled baking sheet in a 375° F. oven for 30 to 35 minutes or until tender. Let cool, peel, seed, and mash.

In a large bowl proof the yeast in the orange juice with the sugar for 15 minutes or until foamy. Scald the milk, add the currants, and let cool.

In a bowl combine the milk and currants, 1 cup of the mashed butternut squash, the brown sugar, butter, egg, orange peel, salt and spices and add the mixture to the

30

yeast. Stir in the flour, 1 cup at a time, to form a soft dough. Knead on a floured surface, incorporating more flour if necessary, for 8 to 10 minutes or until smooth. Put the dough in a bowl coated with butter, turn it to coat with the butter. Cover the bowl with plastic and a dish towel and let the dough rise for 1½ hours or until doubled in bulk.

Punch the dough down, knead it lightly, and divide it in half. Roll each half into a rope 24 inches long and cut each rope into 12 pieces. Form each piece into a ball, arrange about 2 inches apart on oiled baking sheets, and let rise, covered loosely, for 30 to 45 minutes or until almost doubled in bulk. Brush with the glaze and bake in a 375° F. oven for 12 to 15 minutes, or until the rolls sound hollow when the bottoms are tapped. Let cool on racks for 10 minutes. Makes 24.

These spice buns are too good to be reserved solely for holidays. As they are just as flavorful if not more so the day after, suggest toasting them for breakfast accompanied by mounds of softened sweet butter. What better way to begin Easter Sunday celebrations!

Hot Cross Buns

2 tablespoons active-dry
  yeast
3/4 cup lukewarm milk
1/4 cup light brown sugar
2 eggs, beaten lightly
6 tablespoons unsalted
  butter, softened
3/4 teaspoon salt
1 teaspoon cinnamon
1/2 teaspoon freshly
  grated nutmeg
1/4 teaspoon ground
  cloves

1/4 teaspoon allspice
4 to 41/2 cups all-purpose
  unbleached flour
1/2 cup currants or
  raisins or a
  combination of both
An egg wash made by
  beating 1 egg with 2
  teaspoons water and a
  pinch of salt
1/3 cup confectioner's
  sugar
2 to 3 teaspoons milk

In a large bowl proof the yeast in the milk with a teaspoon of the sugar for 15 minutes or until foamy. Stir in
the remaining sugar, the eggs, butter, salt, cinnamon,
nutmeg, cloves, and allspice. Add the flour, 1 cup at a
time, stirring, until the dough is soft and slightly sticky.
Knead the dough on a lightly floured surface for 8 to 10
minutes, or until it is smooth and elastic. Put the dough
into a buttered bowl and turn it to coat with the butter.
Cover the bowl with plastic wrap and a dish towel and
let the dough rise for 1 to 11/2 hours, or until it has
doubled in bulk.

Punch down the dough, flatten it into a rectangle about
1/2 inch thick, and sprinkle the top with the currants.
Roll the dough up into a 21-inch log and cut it crosswise
into 16 pieces. Form the pieces into buns and arrange
them seam side down on lightly buttered and floured
baking sheets. Let the buns rise, covered loosely, until
they have almost doubled in bulk, and brush them with
the glaze. With a sharp knife or razor cut a cross into

the top of each and bake the buns in a 425° F. oven for 15 minutes, or until they sound hollow when their bottoms are tapped. Transfer the buns to racks to cool.

In a small bowl beat the confectioner's sugar with the milk until it forms a thick icing. Drizzle the icing into the crosses on tops of buns. Makes 16 buns.

———

This is a particularly moist quick bread which could easily double as a morning coffee cake. It keeps well if wrapped in plastic and kept in a cool, dark place.

Apricot Pecan Bread

1 cup dried apricots, soaked in warm water for 30 minutes and drained
3 tablespoons unsalted butter, softened
1 cup sugar
1 egg, beaten lightly
1/2 cup sour cream
1/2 cup orange juice
1 1/2 teaspoons grated orange peel

2 cups all-purpose flour
2 teaspoons baking powder
1 teaspoon baking soda
1 teaspoon salt
1 teaspoon cinnamon
1/4 teaspoon freshly grated nutmeg
1 cup chopped pecans

Butter and flour a 9 × 5 × 2 3/4-inch loaf pan. Chop the apricots. Cream the butter, add the sugar, egg, sour cream, orange juice, and orange peel and beat the mixture until it is combined well. Sift the flour, baking powder, baking soda, salt, cinnamon, and nutmeg. Add the dry ingredients to the egg mixture, stirring until just combined. Fold in the apricots and nuts. Pour into the prepared pan and bake in a 350° F. oven for 50 minutes to 1 hour, or until a knife inserted in the center comes out clean. Let the bread cool in the pan on a rack for 10 minutes, invert it onto the rack to remove, and let cool completely. Makes 1 loaf.

A slight change of pace from the more traditional corn breads, this one is especially good with braised meats and stews. It can be kept, covered and chilled, overnight and reheated, wrapped in foil, in a 350° F. oven for 15 minutes or until warm.

Chili Cheese Corn Bread

1 cup yellow cornmeal
1 cup flour
1 teaspoon sugar
1 teaspoon salt
2 eggs
1 cup milk
1 cup corn kernels
6 tablespoons unsalted
butter, melted and
cooled
2 tablespoons minced
onions or scallion
1 to 2 pickled jalapeño
peppers, minced
1 1/2 cups grated sharp
Cheddar cheese

Sift the cornmeal, flour, sugar, and salt. In a bowl combine the eggs, milk, corn, 4 1/2 tablespoons of the butter, the onions and peppers. Stir into the cornmeal mixture just until combined. Fold in 1 1/4 cups of the cheese. Pour the batter into a hot buttered 9-inch cast iron skillet or baking pan, sprinkle the top with the remaining cheese and drizzle it with the remaining butter. Bake in a 425° F. oven for 25 to 30 minutes, or until a knife inserted in the center comes out clean. Let cool in the skillet on a rack for 5 minutes, invert onto the rack to remove, and cool for 5 minutes more.

Delicious companions to simmering winter soups, these scones will keep, covered and chilled, overnight. Simply wrap in foil and reheat in a 350° F. oven for 15 minutes or until warm.

Scallion Cheddar Cheese Scones

2 tablespoons unsalted butter

1/3 cup minced scallions, including green tops

2 1/4 cups all-purpose flour

2 teaspoons baking powder

1 teaspoon salt

1/8 teaspoon cayenne pepper

4 tablespoons unsalted butter, melted and cooled

1 large egg

3/4 cup half and half

1 cup plus 2 tablespoons grated sharp Cheddar cheese

An egg wash made by beating 1 egg with 2 teaspoons water and a pinch of salt

Melt the 2 tablespoons of butter and add the scallions to soften; let cool for 5 minutes. Sift the flour, baking powder, salt, and cayenne into a bowl. Add the 4 tablespoons of butter and cut into the mixture until it resembles coarse meal. In a bowl combine the scallions, egg, and half and half. Stir the scallion mixture into the dry ingredients and fold in 1 cup of the cheese. Form the dough into a ball, flatten it into a round 3/4 inch thick, and transfer to a buttered and floured baking sheet. Brush the dough with the glaze and sprinkle with the remaining cheese. Score the top into 8 wedges and bake in a 425° F. oven for 13 to 15 minutes or until golden. Transfer to a rack and cool for 5 minutes. Makes 8 scones.

Bake these muffins during the blueberry season when the berries are at their best. Covered and chilled, they can be kept overnight and reheated, wrapped in foil, until warm.

Sour Cream Blueberry Muffins

2 cups all-purpose flour
1/2 cup plus 2 tablespoons sugar
2 teaspoons baking powder
1 teaspoon salt
1/2 teaspoon baking soda
1/2 teaspoon cinnamon
1 cup sour cream

1 large egg
4 tablespoons unsalted butter, melted and cooled
1 teaspoon grated orange peel
1/2 teaspoon vanilla extract
1 cup blueberries

Into a bowl sift the flour, reserving 2 tablespoons, and 1/2 cup of the sugar, the baking powder, salt, baking soda, and 1/4 teaspoon of the cinnamon. In another bowl combine the sour cream, egg, butter, orange peel, and vanilla. Toss the blueberries with the reserved flour. In a small bowl combine the remaining sugar and cinnamon. Stir the sour cream mixture into the flour until the batter is just combined, and fold in the blueberries. Spoon the batter into a buttered 12-cup muffin tin, filling 2/3 full. Sprinkle the tops with the cinnamon sugar and bake in a 400° F. oven for 15 to 20 minutes or until the tops are golden brown and a wooden toothpick inserted in the centers comes out clean. Makes 12 muffins.

CAKES, SMALL CAKES,
AND COOKIES

Sturdy cardboard boxes are the best receptacles for transporting and presenting the buttercream cakes included here. Wrap the boxes in gift paper or cover with cutouts and stencils and tie closed with ribbon, yarn, or string. For a more elaborate gift include the serving plate—glass, china, or silver; all would make lovely accompaniments.

The fruitcakes may be wrapped in clear cellophane and decorated with satin ribbon.

Mound cupcakes and brownies on a serving plate, enclose the whole, plate and all, in a large sheet of colorful cellophane, and gather the ends above the top of the mound. Twist and tie with ribbon or string.

Cookies will remain freshest if stored in airtight containers. A fanciful presentation, however, is to layer them in clear glass ginger-type jars festooned with ribbons.

*If hazelnuts are difficult to find, walnuts may be substi-
tuted. This cake keeps well in the refrigerator for several
days. Be sure to bring to room temperature before serving,
so that the buttercream has an opportunity to soften and
develop flavor.*

Hazelnut Mocha Cake

1¼ cups skinned and
    toasted hazelnuts, plus
    8 to 10 for decoration
4 eggs, separated
¾ cup sugar
1 tablespoon dark rum

1 teaspoon vanilla
⅓ cup all-purpose flour,
    sifted
5 tablespoons unsalted
    butter, melted and
    cooled

For the buttercream:
4 egg yolks
½ cup sugar
⅓ cup water
1 cup unsalted butter,
  softened slightly

1 tablespoon instant
    coffee dissolved in 1
    tablespoon hot water
1 to 2 tablespoons dark
    rum

For the sugar syrup:
¼ cup sugar
¼ cup water

2 tablespoons rum, or to
    taste

Butter a 9-inch cake pan, line it with wax paper and
butter the paper. Coat with flour, shaking out the excess.

In a processor or blender grind the hazelnuts fine.
Remeasure 1 cup and set aside the remaining ground
and whole hazelnuts for decoration.

With an electric mixer, beat the egg yolks until combined. Add ½ cup of the sugar, a little at a time, and

beat the mixture until it forms a ribbon. Beat in the rum and vanilla. Beat the egg whites until they form soft peaks. Add the remaining sugar, a little at a time, and beat to stiff peaks. Fold the whites into the yolk mixture alternately with the 1 cup ground hazelnuts, a third at a time. Fold in the flour and the butter. Spoon the batter into the pan and bake the cake in a 350° F. oven for 40 to 45 minutes, or until a cake tester inserted in the center comes out clean. Let cool in the pan on a rack for 10 minutes, then invert pan onto rack to remove cake and let it cool completely.

Make the buttercream: In the bowl of an electric mixer, beat the yolks until combined. In a small heavy saucepan combine the sugar and water, bring to a boil while stirring, and boil until the syrup forms a thread or a candy thermometer registers 224° F. With the mixer running, add the sugar syrup in a stream and beat until the mixture is cool. Add the butter a little at a time and beat until combined well. Beat in the coffee flavoring and rum. Chill until firm but still spreadable.

Make the sugar syrup: Dissolve the sugar in the water, stirring over moderate heat. Cool and stir in the rum.

Split the cake into two layers, drizzle the cut sides with the sugar syrup and spread a layer of the frosting on the bottom half. Cover with the top, spread top and sides with frosting, and press the reserved ground hazelnuts around the sides of the cake. Transfer any remaining frosting to a pastry bag fitted with a decorative tip and pipe rosettes around the edge of the cake. Top each rosette with a whole hazelnut. The cake will keep in the refrigerator for up to 3 days. Let sit at room temperature for at least 15 minutes before serving.

Edouard de Pomiane in his Cooking with Pomiane *recounts a lovely childhood remembrance centered around the present-day Bûche de Noël or Yule Log. It seems his parents had unexpected visitors one year during the Christmas holidays—a gentleman from Spain and his wife, who was from the south of France. They arrived bearing, among other things, a wonderful cake. "As for the good lady, she told us that on Christmas Eve everyone, before going to midnight mass, sent a log to the house where they were invited, to ensure a roaring fire. Perhaps that is the origin of this cake, which one sees in the windows of all the pastry cooks in France at Christmas time and at the New Year." Whatever its origins, I cannot think of a more beautiful gift to give to a friend and her family for the holidays.*

Bûche de Noël (Yule Log)

3 eggs
2 egg yolks
1/2 cup sugar
1/2 teaspoon vanilla
    extract
1 1/2 teaspoons grated
    orange peel

1 cup sifted all-purpose
    flour
1/8 teaspoon salt
4 tablespoons unsalted
    butter, melted and
    cooled

For the sugar syrup:
1/4 cup sugar
1/4 cup water

2 to 3 tablespoons
    Grand Marnier

For the buttercream:
4 egg yolks
1/2 cup sugar
1/4 cup water

1 1/2 cups unsalted
    butter, softened
    slightly

40

| 2 tablespoons Grand Marnier | chocolate, melted and cooled slightly |
| 5 ounces unsweetened | |

Sifted confectioner's sugar and meringue mushrooms for decoration (see page 69)

Butter a jelly-roll pan, line it with wax paper and butter the paper. Sprinkle the paper with flour, shaking off the excess. In a large bowl combine the eggs, yolks, and sugar and whisk the mixture over low heat until it is lukewarm. Off the heat, beat the mixture until it forms a ribbon, then beat in the vanilla. Sift together the flour and the salt. Fold the mixture into the yolks, 1/3 cup at a time, being careful not to overmix. Fold in the butter. Spoon the batter into the prepared pan, smoothing it into an 11 × 16-inch rectangle, and bake in a 425° F. oven for 8 to 10 minutes, or until a cake tester inserted in the center comes out clean. Let the cake cool in the pan on a rack, covered with a dampened dish towel.

Make the sugar syrup: In a saucepan combine the sugar and water, bring the liquid to a simmer, stirring, and simmer until the liquid is clear. Let the syrup cool, then stir in the Grand Marnier.

Make the buttercream: In the bowl of an electric mixer, beat the yolks until combined. In a small heavy saucepan combine the sugar and water, bring the liquid to a boil, and boil until the syrup forms a thread or a candy thermometer registers 224° F. With the mixer running, add the sugar syrup in a stream and beat until the mixture is cool. Add the butter, a little at a time, and beat until combined well. Beat in the Grand Marnier and chocolate.

Invert the cake onto a piece of wax paper, peel off the lining paper, and brush the cake with the sugar syrup. Spread with a layer of buttercream, leaving a 1-inch border on all sides. Beginning with the long side nearest you and lifting the cake with the wax paper, roll up the cake. Trim the ends, cutting them diagonally, and with a spatula spread the remaining buttercream over the cake in an even layer. Pull the tines of a fork down the length of the log to simulate bark, sprinkle very lightly with confectioner's sugar to simulate snow, and decorate with meringue mushrooms, if desired. The cake will keep for several days in the refrigerator. Let stand at room temperature for at least 15 minutes before serving.

Nutritious and yet rich enough to be part of a birthday celebration, make these for that very special little someone in your life.

Peanut Butter Cupcakes

1/2 cup softened unsalted butter

1/2 cup crunchy peanut butter

11/4 cups firmly packed light brown sugar

2 eggs

11/2 teaspoons vanilla

2 cups all-purpose flour

21/2 teaspoons baking powder

1 teaspoon cinnamon

1/2 teaspoon nutmeg

1/2 teaspoon salt

1 cup milk

Chopped peanuts as a garnish (optional)

For the frosting:

1/2 cup crunchy peanut butter

1/2 cup softened unsalted butter

11/2 teaspoons vanilla

5 tablespoons heavy cream

3 cups sifted confectioner's sugar

With an electric mixer, cream the butter with the peanut butter in a large bowl. Add the sugar and beat until light. Add the eggs, one at a time, and the vanilla and beat until combined.

Sift together the flour, baking powder, cinnamon, nutmeg, and salt. Add the dry ingredients alternately with the milk to the peanut butter mixture, stirring until just combined. Spoon the batter into 24 cups of paper-lined muffin tins, filling them 2/3 full, and bake in a 375° F. oven for 25 to 30 minutes. Let the muffins cool.

Make the frosting: With an electric mixer, cream the peanut butter with the butter in a large bowl, add the cream and vanilla and beat until combined. Add the sugar, 1/2 cup at a time, and beat the frosting until it is fluffy. Top the muffins with the frosting and garnish with the chopped peanuts, if desired. Makes 24.

These are delicate butter cookies, sandwiched with apricot jam. The filling can be changed to suit your fancy—raspberry jam or plum preserves would do just as well. The cookies keep well in airtight containers for up to 2 weeks. A good thought for Valentine's Day.

Apricot Hearts

1 cup unsalted butter, softened

1/2 cup sugar

1 teaspoon grated lemon peel

1 teaspoon vanilla

1/4 teaspoon salt
2 cups all-purpose flour, sifted
1 cup apricot preserves

Sifted confectioner's sugar for sprinkling the cookies

Cream the butter with the sugar. Add the lemon peel, the vanilla and the salt. Add the flour, a little at a time, and blend until just combined. Chill the dough wrapped in wax paper for at least 30 minutes. Roll out the dough between sheets of wax paper to a thickness of about 1/8 inch. With a heart-shaped cookie cutter dipped in flour, cut out hearts and arrange 1 inch apart on buttered baking sheets. Bake at 325° F. for 15 minutes or until pale gold. Transfer to racks to cool. Heat the apricot preserves until melted, let cool slightly and spread on half the cookies. Top with the remaining cookies and sprinkle with confectioner's sugar. Store in airtight containers. Makes about 28 cookies.

A collection of recipes for gift giving would not be complete without at least one recipe for traditional Christmas cutout cookies. A festive presentation for these might be to string them with narrow red and green ribbons and arrange them in colorful tin boxes lined with paper doilies.

Speculaas or St. Nicholas Cookies

3/4 cup softened unsalted butter

1/4 cup vegetable shortening

1/2 cup firmly packed light brown sugar

1/2 cup sugar

2 1/2 cups all-purpose flour

1/2 cup finely ground almonds

2 teaspoons baking powder

2 teaspoons cinnamon

1/2 teaspoon salt
1/2 teaspoon freshly
  grated nutmeg

1/4 teaspoon ground
  cloves
1/4 cup heavy cream

For the icing:
1/2 pound sifted
  confectioner's sugar
1 large egg white, beaten
  until foamy

1 to 2 teaspoons white
  vinegar

Cream the butter and shortening with both sugars. Sift the flour, almonds, baking powder, cinnamon, salt, nutmeg and cloves. Add the dry ingredients to the butter mixture alternately with the cream and form the mixture into a ball. Divide the dough in half, wrap in wax paper, and chill overnight.

Roll out the dough, half at a time, between sheets of lightly floured wax paper. With cookie cutters in Christmas shapes, dipped in flour, cut out and arrange 1 inch apart on lightly buttered baking sheets. Bake in a 350° F. oven for 8 to 10 minutes or until firm to the touch. Cool cookies on the sheets on racks for 10 minutes and transfer to racks to cool completely.

Make the icing: Beat the sugar with the egg white until combined, add the vinegar and beat until smooth and stiff. Transfer to a pastry bag fitted with a small plain tip and decorate the cookies. Makes about 3 dozen.

IF STORED IN AIRTIGHT CONTAINERS, THESE CAN BE BAKED WEEKS AHEAD; THEY ONLY DEVELOP IN FLAVOR WITH AGING.

Deliciously chewy, macaroon rosettes complement after-dinner coffee exceptionally well. Charming in appearance, it would be a shame to hide them. Arrange them in layers in a clear glass ginger or apothecary jar sealed with a pretty ribbon or bow.

Macaroon Rosettes

8 ounces pure almond
  paste
1 cup confectioner's
  sugar
1/4 cup granulated sugar
2 egg whites

1 teaspoon vanilla
  extract
1/4 teaspoon almond
  extract
10 glacéed cherries

In a food processor or blender puree the almond paste until of an even texture, add the sugars and puree until combined. With the motor running add the egg whites and vanilla and almond extracts and process until smooth.

Line a baking sheet with parchment paper. Transfer the batter to a pastry bag fitted with a large star tip and pipe

48

1-inch rosettes onto the baking sheet, an inch apart. Cut the cherries into small pieces and arrange 1 piece at the center of each rosette. Bake in a 325° F. oven for 20 minutes or until the cookies are pale golden. Let the cookies cool on the baking sheet for 10 minutes, then transfer to airtight containers. Makes about 4 dozen.

THESE COOKIES WILL KEEP UP TO TWO WEEKS.

An old-time favorite—perfect for picnics, lunch boxes, or as an afternoon snack.

Butterscotch Brownies

1 cup all-purpose flour
2 teaspoons baking
  powder
1 teaspoon salt
1/2 cup unsalted butter

1 cup firmly packed light
  brown sugar
1 egg, lightly beaten
1 1/2 teaspoons vanilla
3/4 cup chopped nuts

Sift flour with baking powder and salt. In a heavy saucepan melt butter over low heat, stir in sugar, a little at a time, and continue to stir the mixture until the sugar is dissolved. Let cool 5 minutes. Stir in egg, flour mixture, vanilla, and nuts. Pour into a buttered 8-inch-square baking pan and bake in a 350° F. oven for 20 to 25 minutes or until a knife inserted in the center comes out clean. Let cool in the pan. Makes about 20 2-inch squares.

PIES AND TARTS

Except for the cranberry sour cream pie, the pumpkin pecan chiffon pie, and the individual mincemeat pies, which can be prepared in advance and will keep well if covered and chilled, the remaining goodies in the selection are best eaten on the day prepared.

The same tips for gift wrapping with care apply here as in the previous chapter, on cakes.

In my opinion this is the classic American dessert, reminding me of church bazaars and community fairs. When prepared well, there is nothing quite so sublime.

Lemon Meringue Pie

For the shell:

1½ cups all-purpose flour

2 teaspoons sugar

¼ teaspoon salt

½ cup cold unsalted butter, cut into bits

2 tablespoons vegetable shortening

3 to 4 tablespoons ice water

¼ teaspoon vanilla

For the filling:

¾ cup sugar

5 tablespoons cornstarch

1 tablespoon grated lemon peel

½ cup lemon juice

¼ teaspoon salt

3 egg yolks

1½ cups simmering milk

2 tablespoons unsalted butter

½ teaspoon vanilla

For the meringue:

3 egg whites, at room temperature

⅛ teaspoon salt

¾ cup sugar

½ teaspoon vanilla

Sifted confectioner's sugar

Make the shell: Combine the flour, sugar, and salt, and cut in the butter and shortening until the mixture resembles coarse meal. Add 3 tablespoons of the ice water, add the vanilla, and toss the mixture until the liquid is incorporated, adding more water if necessary. Form the dough into a ball, flatten the ball slightly, wrap in plastic, and chill for 30 minutes. Roll out the dough into a 1/8-inch-thick round, fit it into a 9-inch piepan, and crimp the edge decoratively. Prick the shell lightly with a fork, line it with wax paper, and fit a smaller piepan into the shell or fill it with beans or rice to weight it down. Bake the shell on a baking sheet in the lower third of oven at 400° F. for 15 minutes. Remove the pan and paper and bake the shell for 10 minutes more, or until it is pale golden. Let cool in the pan on a rack.

Make the filling: In a stainless steel or enameled saucepan combine the sugar, cornstarch, lemon peel, lemon juice, and salt. Add the yolks one at a time, beating well after each addition, and stir in the milk in a stream and the butter. Bring to a boil, stirring, and simmer, stirring, for 2 to 3 minutes or until thickened. Remove the pan from the heat, stir in the vanilla, and let the mixture cool for 5 minutes. Spoon the mixture into the shell, smoothing the top, and let it cool to room temperature.

Make the meringue: In a large bowl beat the egg whites with the salt until soft peaks form, add the sugar a little at a time, and beat until stiff. Beat in the vanilla. Decoratively spoon or pipe the meringue over the filling, covering it completely and sealing the edges. Lightly sift confectioner's sugar over the top and bake in a 350° F. oven for 15 minutes, or until top is pale gold.

*Ginger and pears seem to have an affinity for each other.
In this case the custard is very delicately flavored with
crystallized ginger—enough to delight without being dis-
tracting.*

Gingered Custard Pear Tart

For the shell:
(Same as for Lemon
    Meringue Pie)

For the filling:

4 cups water
2 cups sugar
2 (1 × 3-inch) strips
    lemon peel
1 stick cinnamon
3 whole cloves
5 pears, peeled and
    rubbed with lemon
    juice
3/4 cup heavy cream

1/2 cup sugar
1/4 cup minced
    crystallized ginger
2 eggs
2 egg yolks
1 1/2 teaspoons vanilla
Freshly grated nutmeg to
    taste
Sifted confectioner's
    sugar for garnish

Prepare the dough as for Lemon Meringue Pie, fit it
into a 10-inch tart pan with a removable bottom, and
chill while preparing the custard.

Combine the water, sugar, lemon peel, cinnamon, and
cloves in a large saucepan. Bring to a boil, stirring until
the sugar dissolves. Reduce heat, cover, and simmer 5
minutes. Add the pears to the syrup, cover and simmer,
turning occasionally, for 15 to 20 minutes or until
tender when pierced at the bottom. With a slotted
spoon transfer pears to a baking sheet and bake in a
400° F. oven for 5 minutes to dry. Let cool.

54

In a saucepan scald the cream with the sugar and ginger. Transfer the mixture to a blender and blend until smooth. Add the eggs, yolks, vanilla, and nutmeg and blend just until combined.

Halve lengthwise four of the pears and core each half. Arrange the halves cut side down in the shell with the tops meeting at the center of the tart. Quarter and core the remaining pear and arrange it in between the pear halves. Pour the custard over the pears and bake the tart on a baking sheet in the lower third of oven at 350° F. for 20 to 30 minutes, or until a knife inserted in the center comes out clean. Let the tart cool for 10 minutes and sprinkle it with the confectioner's sugar.

As wonderful as it is, a little bit of mincemeat pie seems to go a long way. These small individual pies are similar to ones I was given while in England. They seem to be large enough to satisfy without your overindulging. They also make lovely gifts and store beautifully.

Individual Mincemeat Pies

For the pastry:

3 cups all-purpose flour
3/4 teaspoon salt
3/4 cup cold unsalted butter, cut into bits

5 tablespoons vegetable shortening
6 tablespoons ice water

3 cups prepared mincemeat
Rum, sherry, or cognac to taste (optional)
An egg wash made by

beating an egg yolk with 2 tablespoons heavy cream
1/4 cup sugar

Sift the flour and salt into a large bowl and cut in the butter and shortening until the mixture resembles coarse meal. Add the water, toss the mixture, and form it into a ball. Halve the dough, wrap in wax paper, and chill for 30 minutes. Sprinkle the mincemeat with the rum, sherry or cognac, to taste and let it stand for 15 minutes.

Roll out one half of the dough to 1/8 inch thickness and cut out rounds with a 41/2-inch cutter. Fit each round into a 12-cup muffin tin. Divide the mincemeat among the cups and brush the edges of the dough with the egg glaze. Roll out the remaining dough, cut out rounds with a 31/2-inch cutter, and fit each round over the mincemeat, gently pressing it down over the filling and crimping the top crust to the bottom.

In a blender blend the sugar until it is fine.

Brush the top of the dough with the glaze and bake the pies on a baking sheet in the lower third of oven at 375° F. for 15 minutes. Brush with the glaze again and bake for 15 minutes more. Once again brush with the glaze, and transfer to the middle of the oven. Continue to bake the pies for 10 to 15 minutes more or until they are golden brown. Transfer the muffin tins to racks, sprinkle with the sugar, and let cool completely. With the tip of a knife, loosen the pies from the tins; lift out and transfer to airtight containers. The pies will keep, tightly covered in a cool dry place, for 1 week. Makes 12 pies.

A beautiful addition to the holiday dessert cart.

Cranberry Sour Cream Pie

For the shell:
(Same as for Lemon
  Meringue Pie)

For the filling:
1 tablespoon unflavored
  gelatin
1/3 cup lemon juice
2 eggs
2/3 cup sugar

1 teaspoon vanilla
2 cups sour cream
1/2 cup heavy cream,
  whipped to soft peaks

For the topping:
2 cups cranberries
1 1/2 cups sugar
1/2 cup water
1/2 teaspoon cinnamon
1/4 teaspoon freshly
  grated nutmeg

1 1/2 teaspoons grated
  orange rind
4 teaspoons cornstarch
  dissolved in 3
  tablespoons orange
  juice

Make the shell: Prepare the shell as for Lemon Meringue Pie, bake and cool.

In a small pan soften the gelatin in the lemon juice. In the top of a double boiler beat the eggs with the sugar over simmering water for 8 to 10 minutes, or until light and voluminous. Remove top of double boiler. Heat the gelatin mixture until melted, add to the eggs, and beat the mixture until cooled. Beat in the vanilla and fold in the sour cream and whipped cream. Spoon filling into shell and chill until firm.

Make the topping: In a stainless steel or enameled saucepan combine the cranberries, sugar, water, cinnamon, nutmeg and orange rind. Bring to a boil and simmer the mixture for 3 to 5 minutes, stirring, or until the berries are just tender. Bring the liquid to a rolling boil, stir in the cornstarch mixture and cook, stirring, until thickened. Let cool to room temperature, spoon over the filling and chill, covered loosely, until ready to serve.

Since the sour cherry season is so short, this wonderful little fruit is in high demand. There is very little more satisfying on a warm summer's day than cherry pie and homemade ice cream.

Deep-Dish Cherry Pie

For the pastry:

1 1/2 cups all-purpose flour

1/2 teaspoon salt

1/2 cup cold unsalted butter, cut into bits

2 tablespoons vegetable shortening

3 to 4 tablespoons ice water

For the filling:

4 cups pitted sour cherries, reserving 1/4 cup of the juice

2 tablespoons flour

1 cup sugar

2 tablespoons unsalted butter, cut into bits

1 teaspoon cinnamon

1/2 teaspoon freshly grated nutmeg

1/8 teaspoon ground cloves

1 tablespoon lemon juice

1/2 teaspoon grated lemon peel

An egg wash made by beating 1 egg with 2 teaspoons water and a pinch of salt

Make the pastry: Sift together the flour and salt and cut in the butter and shortening until the mixture resembles coarse meal. Add 3 tablespoons of the ice water and toss the mixture until it is incorporated. Form the dough into a ball, adding more water if necessary. Flatten the ball slightly, wrap in plastic, and chill it for 30 minutes.

In a large bowl toss the cherries and juice with the remaining ingredients and let stand, covered, for 20 minutes. Transfer the ingredients to a deep 9-inch piepan. Roll out the pastry 1/8 inch thick, arrange it over the filling, crimping the edges decoratively, and brush it with the egg wash. Cut steam vents in the center of the dough and bake the pie in a 425° F. oven for 30 minutes, or until the pastry is golden and the filling is bubbling. Serve accompanied by ice cream, if desired.

The biscuit topping for this cobbler resembles the cobble-stones from which it was named. Although considered a home-style dessert, I think it easily compares in both appearance and taste with many a fancy dessert that would take double the time to prepare.

Honeyed Orange Peach Cobbler

2 1/4 pounds peaches, peeled, cored, and sliced

1 1/2 teaspoons grated orange peel

1 navel orange, peeled, pith removed, and sectioned

1/4 cup orange juice

2 tablespoons lemon juice

1/4 cup honey

1/4 cup firmly packed light brown sugar

1 1/2 tablespoons flour

1/2 teaspoon cinnamon

2 tablespoons unsalted butter, cut into bits

Melted unsalted butter for brushing the biscuits

For the biscuit dough:

1 1/2 cups all-purpose flour

1 tablespoon sugar

2 teaspoons baking powder

1/2 teaspoon salt

6 tablespoons cold unsalted butter, cut into bits

3 to 4 tablespoons milk

In a large bowl combine the peaches with the remaining ingredients except the melted butter. Cover the bowl and let the mixture stand for 15 minutes.

61

Make the biscuit dough: Sift together the flour, sugar, baking powder, and salt. Cut in the butter until the mixture resembles coarse meal. Toss with the milk and form into a ball. Pat the dough on a floured surface into a 1/4-inch thick round. Cut out the biscuits with a 2-inch round cutter dipped in flour. (There should be 16 in all.)

Spoon the peach mixture into a deep 9-inch piepan or baking pan and arrange the biscuits over it, overlapping them slightly. Brush the biscuits with the melted butter and bake in a preheated 375° F. oven for 50 to 60 minutes or until the biscuits are golden and the filling is bubbling. Serve with lightly whipped cream as an accompaniment, if desired.

A rum-flavored, very light pumpkin pie which can be prepared several days in advance and decorated several hours before serving. The next time you are invited to a communal Thanksgiving feast, make this your offering.

Pumpkin Pecan Chiffon Pie

For the piecrust:

1 cup graham cracker crumbs

1/2 cup ground pecans

1/3 cup sugar

1/2 cup unsalted butter, softened

1/2 teaspoon cinnamon

1/4 teaspoon freshly grated nutmeg

For the filling:

1 1/3 cups pumpkin puree (not canned pumpkin pie filling)

4 eggs, separated

3/4 cup sugar

1/2 cup heavy cream

1 teaspoon cinnamon

1/2 teaspoon salt

1/4 teaspoon ginger	to 2 tablespoons dark
1/4 teaspoon nutmeg	rum
1/8 teaspoon ground cloves	1/2 teaspoon vanilla
1 tablespoon unflavored gelatin softened in 1	Whipped cream and whole pecans for decorating the pie

Make the piecrust: Combine all the ingredients and press the mixture into the bottom and sides of a 9-inch piepan. Bake at 350° F. for 15 minutes and let cool.

In a saucepan combine the pumpkin, egg yolks, 1/2 cup of the sugar, the heavy cream, cinnamon, salt, ginger, nutmeg, and cloves and cook the mixture over moderately low heat, stirring, until it thickens. Heat the gelatin mixture until it is dissolved and stir it into the pumpkin. Chill until cool.

In a bowl beat the whites to soft peaks, add the remaining sugar a little at a time, and continue beating until the whites form stiff peaks. Beat in the vanilla. Stir one fourth of the whites into the pumpkin mixture and fold in the remaining whites. Spoon the filling into the shell and chill until set. Garnish the top of the pie with the whipped cream and whole pecans before serving.

During the winter months when we are somewhat limited in the variety of fresh fruit available, we can fortunately turn to the many dried fruits found on supermarket shelves throughout the country. This tart of contrasting colors and textures should please even the most discerning hostess.

Dried Apricot and Fig Tart

For the pastry shell:
(Same as for Lemon
   Meringue Pie)

8 ounces dried apricots
8 ounces dried figs
1/2 cup dry white wine
1/2 teaspoon vanilla

1/2 cup tawny port
1/2 cup sugar
2 tablespoons unsalted
   butter

For the almond cream:
1 egg
1 egg yolk
2/3 cup granulated sugar
3 tablespoons flour
3 tablespoons cornstarch
1 cup scalded milk
2 tablespoons butter

1 teaspoon vanilla
1/2 teaspoon almond
   extract
1 to 2 tablespoons
   Amaretto, or to taste
1/3 cup ground almonds

For the glaze:
1/2 cup apricot jam,
   sieved

2 tablespoons Amaretto
   liqueur

Make the shell: Prepare pastry as for Lemon Meringue Pie, fitting it into a 10-inch square or round tart pan with removable bottom. Bake and let cool.

In separate bowls soak the apricots with the wine, 1/2 cup water, 1/4 cup of the sugar and 1/2 teaspoon vanilla and the figs with the port, 1/2 cup water, and the remaining sugar for 30 minutes. Simmer the apricots for 30 minutes or until tender; increase heat to high and reduce the cooking liquid to 2 tablespoons. Add 1 tablespoon of the butter, shaking the pan to coat the apricots. Simmer the figs for 30 minutes or until tender, increase heat to high and reduce the cooking liquid to 2 tablespoons. Add the remaining butter, shaking the pan to coat the figs. Let the dried fruits cool.

Make the almond cream: In a bowl with an electric mixer beat the egg and yolk until combined. Beat in the

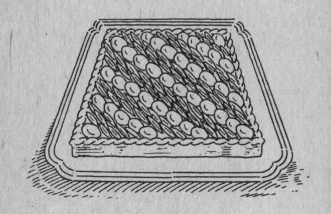

sugar, a little at a time, and beat the mixture until it forms a ribbon. Beat in flour and cornstarch and stir in milk. Transfer to a saucepan, bring to a simmer over moderately low heat, whisking constantly, and whisk the mixture for 2 minutes. Remove the pan from the heat, beat in the butter, vanilla, almond extract, Amaretto, and almonds. Cover and chill until firm.

Spread the tart shell with the almond cream and cover with the fruits, arranging them in alternate rows.

Make the glaze: In a small saucepan, stirring, heat the apricot jam with the Amaretto over moderate heat until syrupy. Brush the fruit with the glaze.

Chill the tart until ready to serve. Let sit at room temperature for 15 minutes before slicing.

CONFECTIONS

My favorite chapter—giving one an indication of the lack of discipline and control I exercise in the realm of caramel popcorn crunch, chocolate truffles, and sugared nuts. Fun to prepare and wrap, almost all these confections improve with age.

Individual gift wraps for these recipes are almost limitless. Aside from decorated tins with tight-fitting lids and jelly glasses and jars topped with fabric, there are tiny berry baskets lined with tissue or fabric, brightly colored cellophane sacks tied with ribbon, clear glass apothecary jars sealed with yarn—not to mention small china, crystal, and silver candy dishes from which to choose. Again, the particular occasion will be the deciding factor as to the costliness of the individual gift wrap.

Piquant and unusual confections, these are delicious as an after-dinner treat with coffee or tea. They may also act as garnitures on ice cream, sherbet, or cake, and are especially good with gelatin desserts.

Candied Citrus Peel

1 large thick-skinned grapefruit	6 cups sugar
2 large thick-skinned navel oranges	1/3 cup corn syrup
	2 cups water

Remove peel with pith from fruit and cut into strips 1/4 inch wide and about 31/2 inches long. Blanch the peel in boiling water three times for 10 minutes each time.

In a heavy stainless steel or enameled saucepan combine 4 cups of the sugar, the corn syrup, and the water. Bring to a boil and simmer for 20 minutes or until syrupy. Add the rind and simmer for 35 to 45 minutes, or until it is translucent and has lost all bitter taste.

Sprinkle the remaining sugar onto a baking sheet lined with wax paper. Working in small batches, drain the peel and dredge it in the sugar. Let the peel dry in a cool, dry place for 24 hours, then pack into containers with tight-fitting lids. Makes about 11/2 pounds.

Charming decorations for cakes and desserts, these little mushrooms are also quite good just to nibble on. Arrange in a tissue-lined berry basket—simulating a miniature mushroom container—and garnish with a calico ribbon.

Meringue Mushrooms

3 eggs whites, at room
   temperature
1/8 teaspoon salt
1/8 teaspoon cream of
   tartar
3/4 cup sugar
1/2 teaspoon vanilla

Sifted confectioner's
   sugar for sprinkling on
   the mushrooms
Sifted unsweetened
   cocoa for sprinkling
   on the mushrooms

Beat the egg whites with the salt until frothy, add cream of tartar, and beat to soft peaks. Add the sugar, a little at a time, and beat until stiff. Beat in vanilla. Transfer all but 1/4 cup of the meringue to a pastry bag fitted with a 1/4-inch plain tip. Set aside the reserved meringue, covered loosely.

Line a baking sheet with parchment or brown paper and pipe onto the paper small rounds of the meringue for mushroom caps and strips for the stems. Sprinkle lightly with the confectioner's sugar and bake in a 275° F. oven for 30 to 35 minutes or until crisp. Remove the caps and stems from the paper and, using the reserved meringue as glue, attach the stems to the caps, gently pushing the stems into the caps. Return to the oven and bake for 10 minutes more, then turn off the heat and let the mushrooms cool completely. Gently dust the mushrooms with the cocoa powder and store in airtight containers. The mushrooms will keep for up to 2 weeks. Makes about 3 dozen mushrooms.

An unusual candy that originated during the seventeenth century in Charleston with the appearance of sesame seeds.

Benne Brittle

Vegetable oil for coating
   the baking pan
3/4 cup sugar

1/2 teaspoon vanilla
3/4 cup toasted sesame
   seeds

Completely coat an 8-inch-square baking pan with the vegetable oil.

In a heavy saucepan melt the sugar over low heat, stirring, until it is clear and amber-colored. Off the heat, stir in the vanilla and sesame seeds. Transfer the mixture to the baking pan, press it into an even layer with the back of an oiled tablespoon, and score it with an oiled knife into 1 to 2-inch squares. When the candy has hardened, invert it onto a work surface and break it where scored into squares. Store in an airtight container. Let sit for at least 1 week before eating. Makes about 1/2 pound.

Wickedly buttery, this popcorn crunch improves with age. A wonderful snack while decorating the holiday tree or watching the last of the season's football games.

Caramel Popcorn Crunch

6 heaping cups popped
   corn
1 pound roasted peanuts
   or almonds
Unflavored vegetable oil
   for coating the bowl,
   baking sheet, and
   spoon

1 1/2 cups sugar
1 cup white corn syrup
1/2 cup water
1 1/2 cups unsalted
   butter, cut into pieces

Combine the popcorn and nuts in a large oiled heat-proof bowl. Have ready an oiled baking sheet or jelly-roll pan and a large wooden spatula coated in oil.

In a heavy saucepan combine the sugar, corn syrup, and water, and bring the mixture to a boil, stirring. Simmer the mixture until the sugar is dissolved. Add the butter and cook, stirring occasionally, until a candy thermometer registers 280° F. Continue to cook, stirring constantly, until the temperature reaches 298°, then immediately pour the caramel syrup over the popcorn and stir to coat the mixture. Pour out onto the baking sheet, flattening into an even layer, and let cool completely. Break into bite-size pieces and store in airtight containers. Makes about 2 1/2 pounds.

Fanciful and slightly romantic, these should be mounded in a clear glass candy dish and could easily act as the finale to a sumptuous meal.

Meringue Kisses

3 large egg whites, at
   room temperature
1/8 teaspoon of salt
1/8 teaspoon cream of
   tartar
3/4 cup granulated sugar
1/2 teaspoon vanilla

1 1/2 teaspoons cognac
3/4 cup semisweet
   chocolate chips
Sifted confectioner's
   sugar for sprinkling
   the meringues

In a large bowl with an electric mixer beat the whites with the salt until they are frothy. Add the cream of tartar and beat to soft peaks. Add the sugar, 2 tablespoons at a time, and beat to stiff peaks. Beat in the vanilla and cognac and fold in the chocolate chips.

Line baking sheets with parchment or brown paper and arrange heaping teaspoonfuls of the meringue 1 1/2 inches apart. Sprinkle lightly with confectioner's sugar and bake in a preheated 275° F. oven for 45 minutes to 1 hour, or until the meringues are firm to the touch. Let cool completely in the oven, then transfer to airtight containers. The meringues will keep for up to 2 weeks if stored in a cool, dry place. Makes about 4 dozen.

Wrapped in colorful cellophane and tied into a garland with narrow ribbon or colorful string, this makes a lovely holiday gift.

English Toffee

2 cups sugar
1½ cups heavy cream
¼ teaspoon cream of
  tartar

10 tablespoons unsalted
  butter
1 tablespoon dark rum

Have ready a shallow baking pan, buttered.

In a large heavy saucepan combine the sugar, cream, and cream of tartar and boil the mixture, stirring, for 3 minutes. Add the butter and boil the mixture, stirring occasionally, until a candy thermometer registers 285° F. Stir in rum and pour into the prepared pan. Let cool until you can make a thumbprint impression in the candy, then with a buttered knife cut into bite-size pieces. Wrap each piece in cellophane or wax paper and store in airtight containers. Let sit for at least 2 weeks before eating. Makes about 1 pound.

These are sinfully rich and delicious. The trick is not allowing the chocolate to overheat. As Chef Jorant of the famous French cooking school La Varenne would say, never allow the chocolate to reach a temperature higher than that of the tip of your tongue.

Chocolate Truffles

10 ounces dark sweet
  chocolate, cut into bits
3 large egg yolks
3 tablespoons heavy
  cream
6 tablespoons softened
  unsalted butter

1 to 2 tablespoons
  Grand Marnier or
  Cointreau
Unsweetened cocoa for
  dredging the truffles

Stir the chocolate in the top of a double boiler set over simmering water until it is just melted. Remove the top from the bottom of double boiler.

In a small saucepan beat the egg yolks with the cream over low heat until the mixture is pale and lukewarm. Remove the pan from the heat and add the chocolate to the eggs, beating until smooth. Add the butter, 1 tablespoon at a time, and the flavoring. Cover the mixture and chill for 1 hour or until firm. Dust the palms of your hands with the cocoa, pinch off heaping teaspoons of the mixture, form into 1-inch balls and dredge them in the cocoa, shaking off the excess. Store the truffles in airtight containers in the refrigerator. The truffles will keep for up to two weeks. Makes about 56.

The wonderful aroma of these confections immediately recalls childhood Christmases.

Chocolate Bourbon Balls

1½ cups ground chocolate wafers

1 cup confectioner's sugar, sifted

1½ cups chopped pecans

¼ cup bourbon, or to taste

2 tablespoons white corn syrup

1 teaspoon cinnamon

½ teaspoon freshly grated nutmeg

Additional confectioner's sugar for dredging the candy

Combine all the ingredients, form the mixture into 1-inch balls and dredge them in sifted confectioner's sugar. Store in airtight containers. These will keep, stored in a cool dry place, for up to 6 weeks. Makes about 4 dozen.

THESE CAN BE PREPARED AHEAD AND ONLY IMPROVE WITH AGE.

As a slight change of pace, serve these with cocktails before dinner, being careful not to put out too many— once tasted, they are difficult to resist.

Cinnamon Sugared Nuts

2 large egg whites
1 teaspoon salt
2 cups sugar
4 teaspoons cinnamon
2 teaspoons nutmeg
1/2 teaspoon ginger
1/4 teaspoon ground
  cloves
1/2 pound roasted nuts
  such as almonds or
  pecans

In a bowl beat the egg whites lightly with the salt. In another bowl sift the sugar, cinnamon, nutmeg, ginger, and cloves and stir until well mixed. Add the nuts to the egg whites, stirring to coat completely, and with a fork transfer the nuts in small batches, being sure to allow the excess egg white to drip off, to the sugar mixture. Dredge completely and arrange 1 inch apart on baking sheets lined with parchment or brown paper. Bake the nuts in a 300° F. oven for 25 to 30 minutes or until the coating is crisp. Let cool for 10 minutes, then store in airtight containers. Makes about 1/2 pound.

This sauce can be served over ice cream or as an accompaniment to cake or Bavarian-type creams.

Minted Chocolate Fudge Sauce

8 ounces dark sweet
  chocolate, cut into bits
2/3 cup heavy cream
2 tablespoons sugar, or
  to taste
3 tablespoons unsalted
  butter, softened

3 to 4 tablespoons
  Crème de Menthe or
  a few drops of oil of
  peppermint or pure
  peppermint extract

Combine the chocolate and heavy cream in a saucepan and cook it over low heat, stirring, just until the chocolate is melted and the sauce is smooth. Add the sugar and cook, stirring, until completely dissolved. Off the heat, stir in the butter and flavoring. Transfer to covered containers or jars and store in the refrigerator. The sauce will keep for up to 2 weeks. Makes about 2 cups.

Homemade sundaes will never be the same after serving this sauce. Particularly good spooned over dark chocolate ice cream.

Maple Pecan Sauce

1⅓ cups pure maple syrup
2 (½ × 2-inch) strips lemon peel
1 stick cinnamon, crushed and broken into pieces
3 whole cloves
½ teaspoon vanilla
⅔ cup chopped pecans

Combine the syrup, lemon peel, cinnamon, and cloves in a saucepan, simmer gently for 5 minutes, add vanilla, and let cool. Strain the syrup into a container, stir in the nuts and store, covered, in the refrigerator. Makes about 1½ cups.

There is nothing quite so sublime as a piece of my friend Virginia Balfour's homemade bread, still warm from the oven, lathered generously with her irresistible maple syrup butter.

Virginia's Maple Syrup Butter

1 quart maple syrup
1 1/2 pounds unsalted
  butter

In a heavy saucepan heat the maple syrup to the soft-ball stage, 234° F., and let cool for 5 minutes. With an electric mixer cream the butter in a bowl, add the maple syrup and beat until light and creamy. Stored in the refrigerator, this butter will keep for up to 6 months. Makes about 6 cups.

Blueberry Syrup

1 pint blueberries (3
  cups)
2 cups sugar
1 stick cinnamon

3 cloves
2 tablespoons lemon
  juice

Combine blueberries, sugar, cinnamon, and cloves in pan with 1 1/2 cups water. Bring mixture to a boil and boil for 10 minutes or until lightly thickened. Strain, stir in lemon juice, and pour into sterilized jars. Serve over ice cream, with cakes, pancakes, and waffles, or in soda. Makes 2 cups.

Cranberry Syrup

3 cups cranberries
2 cups water
1½ cups sugar
1 stick cinnamon,
    cracked

3 whole cloves
2 (1 × 3-inch) strips of
    orange peel
Pinch of salt

In a stainless steel or enameled saucepan combine the cranberries with the water, bring to a simmer and cook over moderate heat, stirring occasionally, until the berries begin to pop. Force the mixture through a food mill or sieve into a large stainless steel or enameled saucepan, add the sugar, cinnamon, cloves, orange peel, and a pinch of salt and gently boil, skimming, for 15 minutes. Strain through a fine sieve into sterilized jars and seal. Makes 2 cups.

PRESERVES AND PICKLES

Probably the most popular gift for giving, the preserves and pickles included here should be prepared according to each season's bounty. Not only will the end results be most flavorful, they will cost a mere pittance to prepare.

Particular attention should be given to the instructions for sterilizing jars, processing them in a water bath and sealing with paraffin. Utmost care must be taken in all of these steps to achieve the highest standards. Be sure all jars are labeled and dated, and give specific instructions for storage.

Ribbon bows with varying patterns are simple and sometimes are the most attractive decorations for the jars. Simply wrap the ribbon around the lid and tie into a pretty bow. Or the lids may be topped with fabric and could be accompanied by a condiment fork or jelly spoon tied onto the jar with a piece of yarn or narrow ribbon. Marmalade pots and crystal jelly jars also make beautiful presentations.

TO STERILIZE JARS OR GLASSES

Wash the jars in hot suds and rinse them in scalding water. Stand them on a rack in a large kettle in hot water to cover, cover kettle and bring water to a boil. Boil jars for 15 minutes, turn off heat and let stand in hot water. Just before they are to be filled, invert jars onto a clean dish towel to dry. Fill while still hot. Sterilize jar lids for 5 minutes, or according to the manufacturer's instructions.

TO SEAL JARS OR GLASSES
WITH PARAFFIN

Fill to within 1/4 inch of the top and fill remaining space with a double layer of melted paraffin.

To prepare paraffin, shave the bar into the top of a double boiler set over simmering water and melt it. When ready to seal the jar, wipe off any jelly that may have stuck to the rim and pour a 1/8-inch layer of the melted paraffin over the jelly, swirling it to cover the jelly completely. Let it set, then pour on another layer of paraffin in the same manner and let it set.

Tomato-Citrus Marmalade

2 pounds tomatoes, peeled, seeded, and chopped

3 cups sugar

1 teaspoon salt

1 orange, sliced thin and quartered

1 lemon, sliced thin and quartered

A cheesecloth bag containing 1 teaspoon whole cloves, 1 stick cinnamon, crushed, and 1 teaspoon dried basil

In a heavy stainless steel or enameled saucepan combine the tomatoes, sugar, and salt. Bring the mixture to a simmer over moderate heat, stirring and skimming the froth, and cook until the sugar is dissolved. Add the remaining ingredients and simmer, stirring occasionally, until a candy thermometer registers 218° F. Remove the cheesecloth bag and spoon marmalade into sterilized jars, filling the glasses to within 1/4 inch of the top. Wipe the rims with a dampened cloth, seal the glasses with paraffin, and let them cool. Store in a cool, dark place. Makes 3 half pints.

Peach Butter

4 pounds ripe peaches, peeled, pitted, and sliced
2 1/2 cups sugar
2 tablespoons lemon juice

A spice bag (1 stick cinnamon, crushed, 6 whole cloves, and 1/2 teaspoon nutmeg tied in a double thickness of cheesecloth)

In a large heavy kettle combine the peaches with 1 cup water and cook, covered, over low heat, stirring occasionally, until the peaches are tender. Force the peaches through the medium disc of a food mill. Return the puree to the kettle, add the sugar, the lemon juice, and spice bag and bring to a boil. Simmer the mixture over low heat, stirring and skimming occasionally, for 1 1/2 to 2 hours or until thick. Spoon into sterilized jars, filling the jars to within 1/4 inch of the top, and rap the jars on a hard surface to eliminate any air bubbles. Wipe the rims with a dampened cloth and seal the jars with the lids. Put the filled jars in a water bath canner or on a rack in a deep kettle and add enough hot water to cover the jars by 2 inches. Bring the water to a boil and process the jars, covered, for 10 minutes. Transfer the jars with canning tongs to a dish towel and let them cool. Store in a cool, dark place. Makes 3 to 4 half pints.

Pineapple Strawberry Conserve

1 pound chopped
pineapple, fresh or
canned
3/4 pound halved
strawberries

3 1/2 cups sugar
1 orange
1 lemon
2 cups toasted almonds,
coarsely chopped

In a heavy stainless steel or enameled saucepan combine the pineapple, strawberries, and sugar. Grate the peel of the orange and lemon into the saucepan and add the juices from the fruits, strained. Bring the mixture to a boil, stirring, and simmer it, stirring occasionally, until a candy thermometer registers 218° F. Stir in the nuts and simmer the mixture, stirring, for 1 minute. Spoon into sterilized jelly glasses and seal the glasses with paraffin. Makes about 4 half pints.

This refreshing relish may be enhanced by the addition of chopped nuts—fold into the relish just before serving.

Orange Cranberry Relish

1 pound cranberries
2 small thin-skinned
oranges
2 small tart apples,
peeled and cored

2 cups sugar
1/8 teaspoon ground
cloves
1/4 teaspoon ginger

In a food processor, meat grinder, or with a sharp knife chop the cranberries until fine. Peel the oranges and mince the rind. Remove the bitter white pith from the oranges and any seeds and chop the flesh. Chop the apples fine. In a bowl combine the cranberries, rind, oranges, apples, sugar, cloves, and ginger and stir the mixture until combined well. Transfer the mixture to jars or containers with tight-fitting lids and let stand in the refrigerator for at least 2 days before serving. Makes about 4 cups.

Seckel Pear Chutney

2 pounds Seckel pears, peeled, cored, and diced
1 onion, chopped fine
2 garlic cloves, minced
2 cups white wine vinegar
1 1/2 cups firmly packed light brown sugar

1 cup raisins
1/2 cup minced crystallized ginger
2 teaspoons salt
1 tablespoon mustard seed
1 teaspoon cinnamon
1/2 teaspoon red pepper flakes

Combine all the ingredients in a large heavy stainless steel or enameled saucepan, bring to a boil, skimming, and simmer, stirring occasionally, for 45 minutes to 1 hour or until the chutney is thick and brown. Transfer to sterilized jars, filling to within 1/2 inch of the top, and process in a simmering water bath (see Peach Butter) for 10 minutes. Store in a cool, dark place. Makes about 4 half pints.

This is delicious with roast meats, poultry, or game.

Red Pepper Jelly

1½ cups minced red
    pepper
1 cup minced green
    pepper
2 to 3 tablespoons
    minced chili pepper,
    or to taste

3 cups sugar
½ cup cider vinegar
¼ cup lemon juice
1 teaspoon salt
3 ounces liquid fruit
    pectin

In a heavy enameled or stainless steel saucepan combine the red pepper, green pepper, chili pepper, sugar, vinegar, lemon juice, and salt. Bring the mixture to a boil, stirring, and boil for 5 minutes. Add the pectin and boil the mixture, stirring, for 1 minute. Pour the jelly into sterilized jelly glasses and seal with paraffin. Store in a cool, dark place. Makes about 4 half pints.

Old-Fashioned Grapefruit Marmalade

2 grapefruit
3 to 4 cups sugar

Remove the rind, cut into thin julienne strips, and peel away the white pith. In a saucepan combine the strips with 1 quart water, bring to a boil and drain. Repeat 2 more times.

Remove the pith from the fruit and section, discarding any membrane. Chop the fruit, saving all juice, and in a large stainless steel or enameled saucepan combine it with the blanched rind and 2 cups water. Simmer 15 minutes. For every 1 cup grapefruit mixture, add 1 cup sugar, bring to a simmer and cook until a candy thermometer registers 218° F., skimming the froth as it rises. Pour the mixture into sterilized jars and process in a water bath (see Peach Butter) for 10 minutes. Store in a cool, dark place. Makes about 3 to 4 half pints.

This is a wonderful way to preserve summer fruits at their best. Combinations are almost limitless—strawberries in kirsch, peaches in rum, cherries in brandy, raspberries in Grand Marnier—whatever appeals most to you.

Spirited Summer Fruits

Fruit of your choice
1 1/2 cups sugar
3/4 cup water

1 vanilla bean, split
1 cup to 1 1/2 cups
    desired spirits

Pack the fruit, peeled and sliced where appropriate, into sterilized jars.

In a heavy saucepan combine the sugar, water, and vanilla bean. Bring to a boil, stirring, and simmer until a candy thermometer registers 230° F. Let cool to room temperature, add 1 part desired spirits to 1 part syrup, and strain over fruits, making sure the fruit is completely covered by the syrup. Seal and store in a cool, dark place.

Deviled Pickled Okra

1 pound small okra
3 cloves garlic, peeled
  and sliced
4 small hot red chili
  peppers
1 cup water

1 cup white distilled
  vinegar
1 1/2 tablespoons salt
1 tablespoon mustard
  seed

Wash the okra, pierce each pod several times with a toothpick, and pack into sterilized jars, dividing the garlic and chili peppers among the jars. In a stainless steel or enameled saucepan combine the remaining ingredients and bring to a boil. Pour the mixture over the okra to within 1/2 inch of the top of the jars and seal the jars with the lids. Process in a simmering water bath (see Peach Butter) for 10 minutes. Store in a cool, dark place. Makes about 4 half pints.

*These sweet-and-sour pumpkin balls complement the
holiday relish tray beautifully. Buying a fresh whole
pumpkin gives you the added bonus of the pumpkin
seeds. Let dry, arrange in an oiled jelly-roll pan, sprinkle
with vegetable oil, and toast in a 350° F. oven, stirring
occasionally, for 10 minutes. Sprinkle with salt, chili
powder, or the seasoning of your choice and bake 5 minutes longer or until crisp. Voilà!—an unusual and inexpensive appetizer to serve with cocktails.*

Spiced Pumpkin Balls

1 medium pumpkin or
    enough to yield 4 cups
    pumpkin balls
3 cups sugar
1 1/2 cups cider vinegar
3/4 cup water
A spice bag (1 stick
    cinnamon, crushed, 8

whole cloves, and 8
whole allspice berries
tied in a double
thickness of
cheesecloth)
2 (1 × 2 1/2-inch) strips
of lemon peel, cut into
julienne strips

Halve the pumpkin, remove the seeds, and with a 1-inch
melon baller scoop the pumpkin into balls. Combine
sugar, vinegar, water, spice bag, and lemon peel in a
large heavy stainless steel or enameled saucepan. Bring
liquid to a boil and simmer 5 minutes. Add the pumpkin
balls and simmer for 10 minutes or until just tender.
Remove spice bag and transfer pumpkin balls to sterilized pint jars, covering completely with the syrup. Seal
and process in a simmering water bath (see Peach Butter) for 10 minutes. Makes 2 pints.

These little pickles are delicious served with cold meats and pâtés.

Pickled Onions

4 cups small pickling onions
1/3 cup salt

3 cups white vinegar
1 cup sugar

Add the onions to a large saucepan of boiling water, bring the water back to the boil, and boil 1 minute. Drain and peel the onions, sprinkle with the salt and chill, covered, overnight. Rinse and drain.

In an enameled or stainless steel saucepan combine the vinegar and sugar. Bring the mixture to a boil, stirring, and add the onions. Bring the liquid back to a boil, then remove the saucepan from the heat and pack the onions into sterilized jars, being sure they are completely covered by the liquid and leaving 1/2 inch headspace. Process the onions in a simmering water bath (see Peach Butter) for 10 minutes. Store in a cool, dry place. Makes about 4 half pints.

CONDIMENTS

Flavored vinegars have recently become quite popular. Simple
and inexpensive to prepare, they make lovely gifts as do compound butters and savory sauces.

Search flea markets and antique shops for unusual-shaped
bottles to house the vinegars. After the vinegars have been
used, the bottles will make charming additions to the pantry
shelf and might even double as decorative accents.

Compound butters are best presented in small glass or porcelain ramekins or in miniature crocks. Covered with plastic
wrap and tied with colored string, they make interesting and
versatile food gifts.

The suggestions for gift wrapping in the previous section
also apply to the savory sauces listed here.

Wonderful in salad dressings, flavored vinegars can also be used to enhance sauces, both hot and cold, and are amazingly easy to prepare. Simply follow the basic procedure below, adding the herbs and seasoning of your choice.

Garlic Chive Vinegar

4 cups cider vinegar
Several stalks of fresh
  garlic chives

2 small garlic cloves,
  peeled

In a stainless steel or enameled saucepan bring the vinegar to a simmer, pour it into a sterilized quart bottle or jar and add the chives and garlic. Store the vinegar in a cool, dark place for at least 2 weeks before serving. Before presenting as a gift, strain and add your favorite fresh herbs to the bottle. Makes 1 quart.

Rosemary Vinegar

1 quart white wine
  vinegar
1 to 2 large sprigs fresh
  rosemary

1 shallot, peeled and
  halved
6 black peppercorns

In a stainless steel or enameled saucepan bring the vinegar to a simmer. Pour it into a sterilized bottle or jar and add the rosemary, shallot and peppercorns. Seal and store in a cool, dark place for at least 2 weeks before serving. Before presenting as a gift, strain and add fresh herbs to the bottle. Makes 1 quart.

Raspberry Vinegar

1 quart white wine
   vinegar

1/2 cup sugar
1 1/2 cups raspberries

In a stainless steel or enameled saucepan combine the vinegar and sugar and bring the mixture to a simmer, stirring. Cook over low heat until the sugar has dissolved, then add the raspberries and gently mash them in the liquid. Transfer to a sterilized quart bottle, seal and let sit in a cool, dark place for at least 2 weeks. Before presenting, strain and add a few fresh berries if desired. Makes 1 quart.

Flavored butters make interesting and welcome gifts. As with the flavored vinegars, they are quite simple to prepare and the possible combinations are almost endless. Serve this butter, softened to room temperature, with grilled or roasted meat and poultry. It can be attractively presented in a porcelain or china ramekin.

Green Peppercorn Butter

1 cup unsalted butter,
   softened
2 tablespoons drained
   green peppercorns
   packed in water
2 teaspoons Dijon-style
   mustard

2 teaspoons lemon juice,
   or to taste
Salt and pepper to taste
3 tablespoons minced
   fresh parsley
3 tablespoons snipped
   fresh chives

In a blender or food processor combine the butter, green peppercorns, mustard, lemon juice, and salt and pepper to taste and blend until smooth. Transfer the mixture to a bowl, stir in the parsley and chives, transfer to a serving dish and store, covered and chilled. Makes about 1¼ cups.

Herb Butter

1 cup unsalted butter,
  softened
3 tablespoons minced
  parsley
2 tablespoons snipped
  fresh chives
2 tablespoons minced
  fresh tarragon

1 tablespoon minced
  fresh chervil
1 teaspoon Dijon-style
  mustard, or to taste
Lemon juice to taste
Salt and pepper to taste

Combine all the ingredients and blend well, adding salt and pepper to taste. Transfer to a serving dish and store, covered and chilled. Makes about 1¼ cups.

Serve this butter on grilled or broiled fish or chicken.

Hazelnut Butter

1 cup unsalted butter
½ cup chopped toasted
  hazelnuts

Salt to taste

Beat the butter with an electric mixer until light and fluffy. Fold in the hazelnuts and salt to taste. Transfer to serving dishes and store, covered and chilled. Makes about 1½ cups.

Sorrel is a deliciously tart herb that is abundant during the summer months. Fortunately it freezes beautifully and can be prepared at its peak and enjoyed throughout the year. The puree can be added as a flavoring to hollandaise and mayonnaise and can also act as an enrichment for cream sauces. It is delicious with fish, poultry, and veal.

Summer Sorrel Puree

1/2 pound sorrel leaves,   4 tablespoons unsalted
   sliced   butter

In a skillet cook the sorrel in the butter over moderate heat, stirring, until it is completely melted. Increase the heat to high and cook until almost all the liquid is evaporated. Puree in a blender or food processor and spoon into a jar or container. Cool, cover, and chill. The puree freezes well and can be kept under refrigeration for up to 1 week. Makes about 1 1/2 cups.

A wonderfully aromatic sauce of Italian origin traditionally served with freshly cooked pasta. Serve the sauce over steamed vegetables, use it as a dressing for pasta salads or as an enrichment in soups. Pesto freezes well and therefore can be enjoyed not only during the summer months, when basil is plentiful, but throughout the year.

Pesto

2 cups basil leaves
2 medium cloves garlic
1/2 cup grated Parmesan
  cheese
2/3 cup olive oil

2 tablespoons unsalted
  butter, softened
1/4 cup pine nuts
1 teaspoon salt
Freshly ground pepper

Combine all the ingredients in a food processor or blender and puree until smooth. Pour into a glass jar or container and chill, covered. Pesto freezes well. Makes about 1 1/2 cups.

This sauce is especially good with smoked seafood, but acts equally well as a salad dressing.

Sour Cream Horseradish Sauce

1 cup sour cream
1/2 cup mayonnaise
1/4 cup undrained
  prepared horseradish
1 small onion, chopped

1 garlic clove, chopped
1 tablespoon lemon juice
1 tablespoon sugar
1 1/2 teaspoons salt
White pepper to taste

Combine all the ingredients in a blender or food processor and blend until smooth. Store, covered and chilled. The sauce keeps up to 1 week in the refrigerator. Makes 2 cups.

98

Orange Plum Tomato Sauce

3 pounds plum tomatoes, seeded and chopped
1 large onion, chopped
1 celery stalk, sliced
2 medium garlic cloves, chopped
1/4 cup olive oil
1/2 cup dry red wine
2 (4-inch) strips orange peel
1 tablespoon brown sugar
1 teaspoon dried basil
1 teaspoon dried thyme
1 bay leaf
1/2 teaspoon dried oregano
1/2 teaspoon fennel seed, crushed
1 teaspoon salt
Freshly ground pepper to taste
4 tablespoons grated Parmesan cheese

In a large saucepan, covered, simmer the tomatoes, onions, celery, and garlic in the olive oil for 8 to 10 minutes or until the vegetables are soft. Add the wine and boil for 1 minute. Add the orange peel, sugar, dried herbs, and salt and pepper and simmer for 1 hour. Force the mixture through the medium disc of a food mill into a saucepan and reduce the sauce to 3 1/2 cups. Stir in the cheese, pour the sauce into a jar or container, let cool and chill, covered. The sauce freezes well. Makes 3 1/2 cups.

This sauce is particularly good for basting spareribs or grilled or broiled chicken. For those who prefer their barbecue sauces devilishly hot, the addition of small green chilies, seeded and minced, or red pepper flakes should do the trick.

Barbecue Sauce

1/2 pound bacon, chopped
2 cups chopped onions
1 green pepper, chopped
4 garlic cloves, minced
1 1/2 cups beef broth
12 ounces bottled chili sauce
1/3 cup brown sugar
2 tablespoons honey
4 tablespoons lemon juice
1 tablespoon grated lemon peel
2 tablespoons cider vinegar

1 teaspoon hot pepper sauce
1 teaspoon salt
1/2 teaspoon cayenne pepper
1/2 teaspoon ground cumin
1/4 teaspoon ginger
1 bay leaf
1/8 teaspoon ground cloves
1 tablespoon Worcestershire sauce, or to taste
3 tablespoons unsalted butter, cut into bits

In a saucepan cook the bacon over moderate heat, stirring, until it is golden. With a slotted spoon, transfer to a plate and pour off all but 2 tablespoons fat. Add the onions and green pepper and cook, covered, stirring occasionally, for 8 to 10 minutes or until the onions are golden brown. Stir in the garlic and cook 1 minute. Add the reserved bacon and all the remaining ingredients except the butter. Simmer for 30 minutes, skimming, and let cool 15 minutes. Discard the bay leaf. Transfer the sauce to a blender and puree until combined well.

With the motor running, add the butter and continue to blend until it is incorporated. Transfer to jars with tight-fitting lids and keep refrigerated. Makes about 4 cups.

BEVERAGES

The spice bags for warm winter drinks may be presented as sachets in clear glass jars and could be accompanied by a bottle of cider, wine, or sherry. An interesting gift wrap for the mocha coffee is a coffee mug or large *café au lait* cup sealed with clear plastic and tied with a ribbon. The syrups and shrubs lend themselves to gift containers similar to those for the vinegars.

The aroma of these little spice bags immediately calls to mind the warmth of an open hearth and the conviviality of friends relaxing after a day of outdoor activity.

Spice Bags
for Warm Winter Drinks

8 sticks cinnamon, crushed and broken into pieces

2 whole nutmegs, crushed

1/3 cup whole cloves

1/3 cup minced dried orange peel or 1/4 cup ground

1/4 cup whole allspice berries

Combine all the ingredients in a bowl, tie in sachets of 1 tablespoon each in a double thickness of cheesecloth, and transfer to an airtight container. One sachet of the mixture will flavor 1 quart of cider or wine. Simply simmer the chosen beverage with a sachet for 20 minutes, ladle into mugs and garnish appropriately with a stick of cinnamon, fresh orange or lemon peel, and perhaps a sprinkling of additional spirits—in the case of a wine punch, sherry; for cider, cognac or rum would be a robust flavoring. Enough for 10 sachets.

Present this flavored coffee in a colorfully decorated tin appropriately labeled with brewing instructions. The finished coffee may be served as is or sweetened. Garnish with lightly whipped cream and a sprinkling of ground cinnamon.

Spiced Mocha Coffee

1⅔ cups freshly ground coffee

¾ cup unsweetened cocoa

2 cinnamon sticks, crushed and broken into small pieces

1 vanilla bean, minced fine

1 teaspoon freshly grated nutmeg

¼ teaspoon salt

Combine all the ingredients, stir to mix, and transfer to an airtight container. Store in a cool, dry place. For each cup of coffee allow 3 tablespoons of the blend. Enough to make 10 cups.

Blueberry Shrub

2 cups blueberries

¼ cup sugar

1 cup orange juice

⅓ cup lemon juice

Put blueberries through a food mill to puree. In a stainless steel or enameled saucepan combine the blueberries and sugar. Bring mixture to a simmer, stirring, and add orange juice and lemon juice. Chill. Serve over crushed ice with seltzer to taste and garnish with an orange slice. Makes 4 drinks.

Grapefruit Shrub

2 cups grapefruit juice
1 cup orange juice
1/2 cup lemon juice

1/2 cup sugar, or to taste
2 tablespoons cider
   vinegar

In a stainless steel or enameled saucepan combine all of the ingredients except vinegar. Bring to a simmer, stirring, and cook until sugar is dissolved. Stir in vinegar. Serve over ice with seltzer to taste. Makes 4 drinks.